Winning Solutions

For

Struggling Readers and Spellers

Simple Sound, Letter and Syllable Lessons for 2nd grade through High School

For Homeschool, Elementary, Middle School, Special Education, Learning Disability,
Dyslexia, Reading Intervention, and ESL Learners
Individualized Reading and Spelling Strategies
With Worksheets, Assessments, Lesson Guide, and Virtual Instruction.
Stressing Development of Phoneme Awareness

Vickie Dinsmore, M.Ed.
Speech Language Pathologist

Winning Solutions for Struggling Readers and Spellers

Front cover image by Vickie Dinsmore

Book Design by Vickie Dinsmore

3rd Revision September 2021

Library of Congress Control Number: 2020920634

Other books in this series

1st "20 Minute Phonemic Training for Dyslexia, Auditory Processing and Spelling"
copyright 2017
ISBN 978-1-5320-2879-3 paperback and ISBN 978-1-5320-2878-6 digital

2nd "Winning Solutions for Struggling Readers and Spellers" Expanded Edition
    of "20 Minute Phonemic Training for Dyslexia, Auditory Processing and Spelling"
copyright 2020
ISBN 9780578780801

3rd ""Winning Solutions for Struggling Readers and Spellers –
Virtual Instruction Edition" Copyright 2021
    ISBN 978-0-578-84882-2

4th "Winning Solutions for Struggling Readers and Spellers – Hardback
    Color Edition   with special notes about virtual instruction. Copyright 2021
    ISBN 978-0-578-84881-5

DEDICATION

To my husband, David, who helped with editing and gave many suggestions.

To my parents, now deceased, who instilled within all five of their children the instinct to pursue their ideas and dreams whether those dreams seemed within reach or not. Their model and successes made it possible for each of us to achieve more than we ever dreamed.

To my sister-in-law Kathi Wittkamper, who encouraged me to write and provided an opportunity for publication of the first book,"20 Minute Phonemic Training for Dyslexia, Auditory Processing and Spelling."

To my family, who listen endlessly to my ideas for struggling readers and spellers.

ACKNOWLEDGMENTS

Thank you to Student A, Student B, and Student C and their families for allowing me the opportunity to write their stories.

Thank you to all the children who taught me as much as I taught them.

Thank you to the readers of "20 Minute Phonemic Training for Dyslexia, Auditory Processing and Spelling" who provided their genuine feedback with ideas for improvements. I hope all your ideas and needs were addressed in this edition.

Table of Contents

Introduction

If you are reading this, then you likely know a child who is struggling to learn how to read and spell. *"Winning Solutions for Struggling Readers and Spellers"* is dedicated to helping you help your student or child overcome reading and spelling challenges. The plan within the following pages is a pathway to reading smoothly and accurately---no more stumbling through the words. Does this sound unbelievable? Type the link below into your computer browser to hear an example of a second semester, 3rd grade struggling reader before and after *"Winning Solutions"* *"20 Minute Phonemic Training"* receiving three months of lessons:

https://youtu.be/7-ErgMoLl80

In the following chapters, you will learn:

A) How to determine exactly which sounds your child can distinguish from other sounds. You will know which sounds are confusing to your child. Vowel tones are especially difficult for many people to tell apart. ("Did I hear a short /i/ or /e/ or /a/? "). Slight differences between similar consonant sounds are also hard to process.("Could that be an /s/ or /sh/? Did I hear an /f/ or a /th/? Is that a /t/ or a /d/ sound?") So, when the struggling reader is writing, he or she does not know which letters to use.

B) Phonic rule letter patterns are determined by sounds that come before the letter pattern is applied or by the position of sounds in words. In this book *you will learn how to show the student how to 'hear' and 'process' the individual sounds and their position in words.* In the chapters that follow you will *learn how to help students know when to use the phonic letter patterns that go with the sounds they hear.*

C) Some children are successful readers when they have pictures, and they can memorize the words. People with strong visual memory know a lot of words on sight. However, around third grade or fourth grade, this skill begins to fail them. Pictures begin to disappear. Words are longer. They see words they may not have heard before, and the sentences are longer too. There are just too many words to memorize on sight!

D) Many people will tell you that the English language is not predictable, and patterns do not occur. In this book you will see the hidden patterns to teach them a way to read longer words with ease. You will learn a technique using prefixes and suffixes to find stressed and unstressed syllables. This system uses vowel tones to establish the rhythm of words. Follow this link to an example: https://youtu.be/FEJgh2KwKZgE)

E) You will learn how to teach each sound and syllable level step-by-step using short, interactive lessons tailored to exactly what your student needs. You will be guided through the four parts of each lesson: 1) hearing each sound in the word, 2) telling the sounds apart, putting the sounds together, 3) reading the written words, and 4) spelling/writing the words. Phonic rules and vowel combinations are embedded within each chain of ten words and vary according to the level your child is learning.

F) Reading practice is provided in the form of leveled short stories and a system for using repetitive reading with phrasing strategies. Once your student understands the sound and letter matches, once your child can 'hear' the differences between the vowel tones, voiced and voiceless sounds, and high frequency sounds, then they will correctly 'map' the sounds to letters. It is at this point the phrase 'sound out the word' will make sense and repeated reading practice will yield faster and more accurate reading.

Who will benefit most?

"Winning Solutions for Struggling Readers and Spellers" will benefit any child learning to read and spell. It is a combined approach for teaching reading and spelling. However, the typical student, who will benefit most, is reading six months to two years or more below grade level, writing little and what they write is not readable due to poor spelling. Math calculations are often an area of strength. This student will likely have a history of language and/or articulation delayed impairment which is often accompanied by a history of middle ear infection, with or without mild, intermittent hearing loss. This child needs instruction that uses eyes, ears, and motor movement with descriptive language to help them sense and differentiate individual sounds [phonemes] in words.

Precious Time Saved Preparing Lessons

"Winning Solutions for Struggling Readers and Spellers" outlines a process that captures a plan you put into action. After you have completed the process to find out what you will teach your child, the lessons become automatic. You will use the word lists and worksheets from the book that apply to the phonemes and letter patterns your child needs to learn. The lessons follow a pattern that is comfortable for you and the student. You will collect progress information as a part of each lesson.

Remember this
The key to any strategy for creating change is that the strategy or plan used:
- must be appropriate to the condition for which it is designed. *[finding the weak points is critical]*
- must be applied. *['saying you will do something' and 'doing 'the plan are miles apart!]*
- must be applied correctly.*[teach them using the strategies provided]*
- must be applied with enough frequency.*[skipping lessons will work against your progress]*
- must be applied with enough time in each lesson
     [giving it a couple of minutes and saying you did it will not work]
  must be applied over a long enough period as appropriate to the severity of the condition
     [it takes more than a week or two]

As with learning any skill {i.e., playing an instrument, shooting hoops, or riding a bike}, listening, remembering, and learning sounds, letter recognition and the relationship of letters to sounds, reading, and writing require adequate exposure through time and practice. Kindly allow yourself and your student adequate instructional frequency and time to develop skills.

A minimum of two thirty-minute sessions per week is recommended. Three sessions weekly is optimal. The actual lesson requires twenty minutes for most students. Thirty minutes allows five minutes for transition into the lesson and another five minute transition for sharing a summary of feedback to the student at the end of the lesson. Giving your student feedback is important for motivation. Forty minutes would also allow for a repeated reading practice. I found that students were eager and asked, "What are we doing today?" and "Why do I have to stop now?" once they began to experience success. Groups of two students are doable.

Specialists in schools may or may not be trained to help students separate, blend, and match sounds with letters. In addition, due to the large number of students they serve, many specialists are strapped for time and ill equipped to meet the needs of the struggling reader and speller. Today, even when specialists do understand how the auditory system connects to reading and spelling development, they face many challenges to find materials and methods to teach 'virtually'.

Over the past 30 years, teaching methods for teaching reading and spelling have moved from one extreme direction to another. One year it was exposure to print and whole word memorization and another it was all about phonics. Today fMri images of brains [1] present a new dimension to research about reading. We now know that before letters in written words can make sense, the spoken sounds in words need to be heard, processed, and sorted for specific differences so children can correctly match sounds to letters in words. If you do not 'get' the sounds, then phonics, reading, spelling, and writing may not make sense!

"20 Minute Phonemic Training for Dyslexia, Auditory Processing and Spelling" was written immediately after I retired. It is now used by tutors and teachers all over the world. Some readers asked for more information on topics barely touched upon in the first book so *"Winning Solutions for Struggling Readers and Spellers"* was written. The intent is to give anyone who wants to help a struggling reader or speller the knowledge and tools I used over the past 30 years to successfully help students.

------

[1] DeHaene, Stanislas, "READING IN THE BRAIN" Copyright © 2009 by Stanislas Dehaene. A study of fMri images of children and adults reading. Images were taken and compared between children before and after learning to read, while reading and those with and without reading disabilities. Conclusions were that the brain is changed by learning to read. Learning to map phonemes to letters, and development of phonological and phonemic awareness skills through direct, sequenced instruction is necessary for successful reading and spelling acquisition.

How is "Winning Solutions" different from "20 Minute Phonemic Training?"

•"*Winning Solutions for Struggling Readers and Spellers*" includes more informal assessments than *"20 Minute Phonemic Training for Dyslexia, Auditory Processing and Spelling"* and explains how to review student writing/reading errors. If you are a detailed individual who likes to receive step-by-step directions, you will like the explanation for how to find out exactly which sounds, letters, phonic rules, and phonemic skills your child still needs to learn. If you are an accomplished specialist, and feel you do not need the in-depth explanations, you will still love the word lists and worksheets included. Lessons are easy to do with minimal materials needed outside of the forms included within the book.

•For anyone unfamiliar with teaching reading and spelling to students who struggle, the reader is guided to know what to do with the information collected from student reading and writing samples by following 4 easy steps. It is important to understand that the book is intended to be read step-by-step. That means you will not read the whole book all at one time. You will read Part 1 for the first step. STOP. Do that step with your child, then Read Part 2. STOP. Do that step with your child and so forth. Detailed directions for following the steps and a description of each step are included at the beginning of Chapter 1.

•In this edition there are more word lists [160 chained word lists and 15 multiple syllable word decoding / encoding worksheets having 8 to 12 words per page with a total of 424 multiple syllable words] for lessons to target student needs with greater precision.

•Answer pages for all worksheets.

•The lesson forms are larger and easier to use than in the first publication.

•Private video links are included demonstrating how to help when students are 'stuck.'

•Informal assessments for reading speed and accuracy [fluency] are included.

•Also included are ***informal assessments*** for

- sound *[phoneme]* blending *[putting sounds together to form words]*, *[k-a-t] =cat*
- segmenting *[separating sounds for the purpose of spelling]*, *cat = [k- a-t]*
- adding sounds *[to make new words]*, *[s + k-a-t=scat]*
- deletions or removing sounds *[to make new words]*, *cat take away /k/ =at and*
- changing sounds. *[to make new words]. "Cat" take out the /a/ and put in an /u/ = cut*

•You will find more information about what to do when your student is not making progress.

•Links to private YouTube videos demonstrating how to use the strategies.

•You will follow three students through their journey from struggling reader and speller to grade level success.

CHAPTER 1

How to Use this Book

There are 4 steps in this approach to teaching reading and spelling. The steps are described and the materials you will need to complete each step are included within the chapter where each step is presented or in Chapter 11. Chapters 2 and 10 describe the journeys of three students through the program. The solutions presented here **supplement** homeschool or classroom reading curriculum and do not replace great literature for developing comprehension and writing.

STEP 1: Read Chapter 1. You will find all materials needed to complete this step in Chapters 1 and 11. Complete step 1 with your child then STOP. Chapter 2 introduces you to three students at the beginning of their journey. Go to Chapter 3 for your next set of directions for Step 2.

STEP 2: Read Chapter 3. You will find all materials needed to complete this step in the book. The tasks you have already completed will provide information about your child that you will use during Step 2. Chapters 3 and 11 will have everything else that you need. Complete this step, which will not involve your child at this time. STOP.

STEP 3: Read Chapter 4. You will find all materials needed for this step in Chapters 4, 6, 7 and 11. You will be referring to the data you have collected. Again, you will not be working with your child just yet. STOP.

STEP 4: Read Chapters 5 and 8. You will find all materials needed in the work you have already done and in Chapters 5, 6, 7, 8 and 11. Now is when you begin to work with your child. You will begin lessons when you have read Chapters 5 and 8. Since you have completed steps 1 and 2, your lessons will be on 'autopilot' for planning and materials used. When your student meets a challenging lesson or task, refer back to Chapter 5 or 8 for information about what to do. When your child is ready for multiple syllable words, you will find all directions and materials for teaching how to read and spell multiple syllable words in Chapters 8 and 9.

Definitions for 'teacher words' and 'speech pathologist' words are underlined in the glossary at the end of the book. For example, titles above word lists in Chapters 6 and 7 include descriptors for location of where sound is produced in the mouth [velars, nasal, labial, etc.] and names for letter combinations [digraph, diphthong, etc.] appear as underlined words in the glossary.

The word 'consonant' means a letter or sound in the alphabet that is not a vowel. Consonants (C) are: [b, p , t, d, k, g, f, v, s, z, sh, ch, j as in judge, l, r, m, n, w, h, ng, th]. Vowels (V) are [a, e, i o, u, [y sometimes] and all the variations of sound they make]. A word like 'cat' has a (C)(V) and a (C) so we write that as 'CVC.' A word like 'scat' is shown as 'CCVC.' The video at this link shows how I explain the difference between consonants and vowels to the children: https://youtu.be/qssRnXu_7Vk

MATERIALS YOU WILL NEED

For Face to Face Instruction

- ✓ Paint daubers, markers OR crayons
- ✓ Flat marbles like a florist might use. Available at many dollar stores--OR small squares of colored paper to use instead of marbles. Cut them in different shapes if your students are color blind.
- ✓ Letter Tiles or letters written on small paper squares. Chapter 11 has letters that you can print and cut apart.
- ✓ Photocopies of the Student worksheets in Chapter 11.
    - One for simple syllables CVC*
    - One for complex syllables CCVC
    - One for complex CVCC
    - One for complex , CCVC
    *See Note Below
- ✓ A Teacher Notes page [Chapter 11]
- ✓ Something to write with such as a pencil, colored pencils, ink pen, or colored ink pens. I find children love having colored gel pens.
- ✓ This book for the wordlists.
- ✓ Other forms included in Chapter 11 as needed.
- ✓ Other forms included in Chapter 11 as needed. *C = Consonant sounds/letters p, b, t, d, k, g, f, v, th, s, sh, ch, j, m, n, ng, r, l, w, h, c, x,V= Vowel sounds/letters i, e, a, o, u, and combinations of letters [ai, ee, etc. see Appendix K]

For Virtual Instruction

- ✓ Copies of both paperback and e-book versions of this text
- ✓ Screen sharing with option to give your student mouse control Or annotation available on your conference platform
- ✓ Open the e-book to the student worksheet your student will need and use the annotate option on your platform.
- ✓ If you are a virtual teacher or tutor AND you wish to have handwritten products, then students will need pencil and paper, and parent will need ability to take a picture of the student's written products and be able to send the photo to you in a text or email.
- ✓ Wordlists from Chapters 6 and 7
- ✓ Open the e-book to any of the Multiple Syllable Word Worksheets from Chapter 9. Use the annotate option on your platform to underline and highlight or add a square over the stressed syllable.

Abraham Lincoln once said, "Give me six hours to chop down a tree, and I will spend the first four sharpening the ax."

President Lincoln knew the tree would fall much faster and with less work if he used a sharp ax rather than a dull ax. Getting that ax ready was just as important as using it to chop down the tree.

When we do not have the right information, the correct tools, enough time or the best methods to help a student, our students' success will be limited if not stopped. Likewise, getting to know how your student perceives words, letters and sounds is more important than teaching a 'prepackaged' list of scripted lessons. When you take the time to learn where student understanding and perceptions are broken, the use of scripted materials becomes more effective. The teacher or tutor is then able to teach to the students' weaknesses using student strengths to motivate and encourage.

While obtaining and reviewing student samples at the beginning of your journey may take as long as two to four hours, the review will give you [and your student] more progress with less time spent in lessons, simply because you are not teaching what your student already knows AND you ARE programming your instruction for student success. When students feel successful, they are motivated and hungry for more.

The process and lessons outlined in *"Struggling Reader Solutions for Struggling Readers and Spellers"* are intended to be used with children in mid to late 2nd grade through high school [or adults], who are failing or have failed to develop reading and writing fluency anticipated for children of their age and grade level [or adults].

The information you will collect may be collected virtually or in person. When collecting virtually, have the student use paper and pencil, then have the parent take a snapshot of the students' work using a cellphone and text the picture to you. If using computer, then use the remote control share option and take a screen shot of your computer screen to save student products.

WHAT: An authentic writing sample is simply something the student writes in their own words. It might be a story about a vacation or a story they make up. It might be a letter to grandma. If you have them write answers on tests, those will do. Anything that they have written AND no one else has corrected, is an authentic writing sample.

WHY: We want to know if the student can write a message, story, or answer to a question that other people can read! While abbreviations in text messages work well for most people; in business, school, and many formal kinds of writing, spelling matters. Lots of children can memorize a list of words for a spelling test on Friday, but do not spell the same word correctly when they use those same words in their writing. Worse yet, children often avoid writing words they do not know how to spell. This leads to writing that lacks depth when writing short messages, answers, and stories.

Spell check has been praised as the answer to poor spelling. However, it is not perfect. The following sentence was checked by Microsoft Word spell check as an example.

There are mane errs that are knot pecked up bye spill chick.
Correctly written: There are many errors that are not picked up by spell check.

HOW: When would you need a writing prompt? How do I use writing prompts? Not often. If your student is writing for you or another teacher, then all you will need is copies of what they have already written. Writing journals, sentence answers to homework or test questions, and drafts of stories they write are all great examples of authentic writing. The important thing to remember is that it must be written by the child before graded for spelling errors or edited by anyone else.

In Chapter 11 there is a list of **Suggested Writing Prompts.** Use these when children avoid writing and it is just too difficult to obtain seventy-five to one hundred words of authentic writing.

When using the writing prompts, take time to talk about the topic the child will write about. Ask them questions, make it a conversational topic to get them to speak their thoughts. Then restate what they have told you to confirm understanding. After the conversation, ask them to write down their ideas or story for you. Tell them they will only need to write for five minutes. If they do not know where to begin, tell them a phrase to write to get them started. Remind them that "this will not be graded, and spelling will not be graded, just write down your ideas and do the best you can."

The collection of samples will help you see how well they match sounds to letters in the right order, and how they apply phonic rules when writing. Remember that you are not sampling their narrative ability.

Word Level Spelling Sample

WHAT: Use the ***Word Level Spelling Assessment informal spelling tests*** found in Chapter 11. The three word lists range from easy to more difficult words with simple syllable words to two syllable words.

WHY. Sometimes people avoid writing words they do not know how to spell, which limits the vocabulary they can use in their writing. Children will often know many more words than they will write because they do not know how to spell them. The words on this list force students to try to spell words that have both short and long vowels in combination with all the sounds and letters in the English language. The lists also contain some of the early, basic phonic rules for spelling words. We will use the information from this assessment to see which sounds and phonic rule letter patterns the student CAN write successfully and which ones they cannot.

HOW: Read the first list of words found in Chapter 11 to the student as a teacher might for a spelling test. If the student spells 70% percent or more of the words correctly, give them the second list. If the student spells 80% on the second list correctly, give the third list.

- The first list samples ability to map sounds to letters and tell the difference between "noisy" [voiced] phonemes [/b/ /d/ /z/ etc.] and "quiet" [voiceless] phonemes [/p/ & /b/ | /t/ & /d/ | /s/ & /z/ | /f/ and /v/ | /th/ as in 'think' & /th/ as in 'them' | /k/ & /g/], short vowel tones /i/ /e/ /a/ /u/ /o/ & long vowel tones, and apply the 'final e' rule to a long vowel.
- The second list samples ability to tell the difference between ALL the sounds AND represent all sounds when they are in blends in words. We will also see if they apply short vowel phonic rules for spelling patterns in one-syllable words.
- The third list looks at whether the student can correctly spell endings and knows when to use 2 consonants when adding a second syllable. This is often referred to as "consonant doubling." Also found on this list are –le syllables in two syllable words.

Many words were chosen to be novel to children to challenge them to think about how to spell the words. If students can write the phonemes correctly, they are probably able to hear the sound differences. Ability to apply phonic rules for long and short vowel tones such as final e rule, floss rule*, or –ck rule may also be analyzed from the samples taken. ***Grids showing the types of sounds*** and their combinations are included in Chapter 11 to show the sounds and letters selected for sampling. *See Phonic Rule Poster in Chapter 11.

Additional resources for the ***shape and position for jaw, lips, and tongue*** are also in Chapter 11. Students often benefit from seeing the location of the jaw and shape of the lips in relationship to the tone of vowel sounds. Therefore, a picture of the vowel tones with a side view of a face is included. Photos of lips with jaw placement are also included for each vowel tone. See https://youtu.be/H_HFX2izaaY for visual demonstration. *Chapter 11 has **worksheets to help you with sorting student errors**.*

Playing with Sounds Sample [Phoneme Processing Skills]

WHAT: The Sound Play Assessment is an informal assessment designed to collect samples of ability to blend [put together sounds], segment [separate sounds in words], delete [remove or leave out sounds in words], insert [add additional sounds in words], substitute [change sounds in words] and reverse sounds when they are LISTENING to words and sounds.

WHY: When children have difficulty sounding out words, it is often because they cannot separate sounds in words or blend them together. In kindergarten and first grade teachers teach children how to identify the first, last and middle sounds in words. They also teach word families and rhyming words.

A problem exists for many children because, for about 20% to 30% of children, words sound like all one sound. Some people cannot, or find it difficult to, separate the sounds in words. Think about when you hear someone speaking another language that is unfamiliar to you. It sounds like the words are running together so you cannot tell where one word stops, and the next word begins. Sounds overlap, but when most babies mature, their brains begin to 'hear' where one word ends and the next begins around ages three to five. When they start school, most children are processing the individual sounds in words. Heather Winskel reported, in the British Journal of Educational Psychology, that an early history of otitis media in children is linked to delays in early language and literacy skill development.[2]   In my own research paper in graduate studies, I also studied the effects of three or more ear infections prior to age three and found similar results using a much smaller sample.

HOW: Complete directions for how to use the Sound Play Assessment are written in each section. Your child will be LISTENING only --No written letters are used. You will quickly see which of the activities the student can do easily, and which activities are hard.

When teaching the mini lessons, the teacher models and students practice the tasks that were hard for them on these samples. When you begin the lessons, you will only use the tasks they can do well when the student needs encouragement. This is to show them that they are good at doing something well with sounds. For example, perhaps a child can blend sounds together well, but segmenting, or separating the sounds within a word is difficult. Then you will give the blending task first to introduce a list and model separating the sounds for the child.

Then when you ask the child to separate the sounds in the words, they will have already been successful with one task, heard the separating task modeled and find doing it themselves to be much easier. As the student 'grows to grade level' in ability to separate the sounds, then stop giving them sounds to blend in your lessons. In Chapters 3,4, and 5 more information will be given to help you know which phonemic awareness skills- **blending** (putting sounds

----

[2] Winskel, Heather The effects of an early history of otitis media on children's language and literacy skill development Article in British Journal of Educational Psychology · January 2007

together to make a word), **segmenting** (separating the sounds in words), **deleting** (taking a sound out of a word to make a new word – scat -> cat), **inserting** (adding a sound to make a new word--bend -> blend), **reversing** (changing the order of sounds to make a new word--carb -> crab) , or **changing** [exchanging one sound for another to make a new word—cat-> cut->cub]) you will want to include in your lessons.

How Fast and How Accurately Do They Read? [Reading Fluency]

WHAT: There are five leveled short stories [see Chapter 11] ranging from first grade to fifth grade in difficulty. There are two copies of each story. One copy is for your child to read and one copy, with numbers in the margin, is for you to use. The numbers make it easy for you to quickly know how many words your child has read.

WHY: Researchers have learned that reading speed, or rate, and accuracy are particularly important to reading comprehension. When you struggle to lift the words from the page, you use so much cognition to read the words, understanding what was read is reduced. Researchers have also learned that reading the same passage repeatedly increases reading rate and accuracy. It is like learning to play a musical instrument or shooting hoops. The more you practice, the easier it becomes and the more accurately you can perform the task. [2] [3]

HOW: We will use the stories in two ways. One is to collect information about how fast your student reads and how many mistakes they make when reading. A second way we will use them is to practice repeatedly reading the stories in mini lessons. [4] For collecting information, you will listen to your student read for 1 minute. You will then calculate how many words per minute they read and the percentage of words they read correctly.

A Fluency calculation page is included in Chapter 11 to show how to calculate how many words per minute your student reads and how accurately they read.

----

[2] [3][4] Fair, Ginnie Chase and Combs, Dorie. "Nudging Fledgling Teen Readers from the Nest: From Round Robin to Real Reading" The Clearing House, 84:224-230, 2011 Copyright Taylor & Francis Group, LLC ISSN: 0009-8655 prin; 1939-912x online DOIL 1).1080/00098655.2011.575417

[2] [3][4] Meyer, Mariane S., and Felton Rebecca H. "Repeated Reading to Enhance Fluency: Approaches and New Directions" Annals of Dyslexia, Vol. 49, 1999 Copyright 1999 by the International Dyslexia Association ISSN 0736-9387

CHAPTER 2

Student A | Student B | Student C

In this Chapter we will look at "pictures" of three students using the information collected as in Chapter 1 prior to receiving "20 Minute Phonemic Training" lessons. This is also an example of how a summary of the information you have collected might appear.

After collecting Student A's story samples, word level spelling sample, sound play activities samples, and reading sample, this is how A's reading and spelling skills appeared.

AGE: 8 Grade: 3. Second Semester Public School K-3 IEP [Individual Education Plan] services in the classroom. [An IEP is written for a student that qualifies for special assistance of any kind in the schools under the federal Individuals with Disabilities Act, sometimes called IDEA. The IEP sets goals for the student to achieve, guides the teachers to focus on specific skills they will teach the child using special approaches, and often gives the students special help with tests.]

School Progress Report end of first semester grade 3:

- *GOAL: Reading lists of 2 syllable words with blends to 85% accuracy* | Student A met the goal per the progress report.
- *Objective: Reading lists of 2 syllable words with open and closed syllables to 85% accuracy on 3 of 4 trials* | Student A met this goal to 80% accuracy per the progress report.
- *Objective: Reading lists of multiple syllable words to 85% accuracy on 3 / 4 trials* | This goal was not introduced.
- *Objective: Reading 2nd grade level text to 38 words per minute on 3 / 4 trials* | Student A read mid-first grade text (Level H) to 26 words per minute per the progress report.
- *Objective: Answering questions about 1st grade level text to 70% accuracy on 3 of 4 trials* | Student A answered questions for beginning 2nd grade level text [Level K] to 70% accuracy per the progress report.

With Intervention Specialist supports in place, student A met and exceeded IEP goals in the last half of 2nd grade and first half of 3rd grade. It should be noted that 3rd grade students in mid to late year are expected to be reading Level P or Q. Therefore, student A continued to require supports to reach grade level fluency, accuracy, and comprehension skill levels.

Parent Information: Mother shared that Student A had struggled with acquisition of reading skills but loved to write. Student A is smart and with IEP supports, grades improved. Student A was doing much better in school in 3rd grade.

Classroom Writing Samples [5] collected from classroom writing during the first semester:

At the beginning of the 1st semester student A spelled 76% and 77% of the words correctly in writing samples. Some words could not be read due to spelling errors. Legible handwriting was used. Sentences and grammar were age appropriate. Student A did not appear to be avoiding words due to spelling difficulty.

NOTE: Fountas and Pinnell and Orton Gillingham instruction was provided in K through 3rd grade.

Word Level Spelling Sample for Student A at the beginning of the 2nd semester by the Speech Pathologist: On the first list [found in Chapter 11], which has all "3 sound" words, Student A spelled 76% or 23 of 30 words correctly. On the second list, which has "4-5 sound" words, Student A spelled 65% or 26 of 40 words correctly. The 3rd list was not given because student scores on the first two lists were below 80% .

1 van	Mixes up lower case b/d d/b	23/30 76%
2 Pit		
3 mix	Phonic: Floss rule Final e rule? maybe	19 feed
4 rod		20 Cut b/d
5 Chum		21 Zit
6 MeSh	Mixes up /f/ and /th/ sounds	22 boS bess t/th
7 Chip	May not hear or process differences between long and short vowel sounds.	23 fed MOI
8 Shut		24 Sun SHEAT/SHEET
9 thug	Some 'remember' or Mental Orthographic Imagery errors for vowels 'ea' used for 'ee	25 niP
10 beff		26 buZ buzz
11 hide		27 lid
12 wave	Appears to be able to distinguish between the short vowel sounds and can match them to letters correctly.	28 bill
13 rode		29 Mut mutt
14 gap		30 Wov wove
15 gape		Cut cute
16 Sheat	23 of 30 words spelled correctly. 76%	
17 Cot		

1 blak
2 brack
3 flake
4 stack
5 track
6 brand
7 snak
8 strand
9 drug
10 snug
11 plut
12 trick
13 chick
14 spend
15 plant
16 split
17 spunk
18 lesd

19 fret
20 crest
21 clunck
22 drynk
23 fling
24 glad
25 print
26 grand
27 crack
28 scood
29 swang
30 slip
31 listes
32 smok
33 husk
34 frunk
35 slunk
36 glad

37 prise
38 grape
39 smak
40 skunk

26/40 correctly spelled for 65%

NOTE: List 3 was not given because scores were too low on the first two lists.

Sound Play Activity Samples:

A small sample of sound blending was obtained with CVC words. It was noted that Student A was not automatic with blending. When sounding out words while reading, this student needed time to process the sounds as the student tried to sound them out.

When asked to segment or separate the sounds in words, Student A had difficulty saying the short vowel sounds correctly and separating the sounds in blends [two consonant sounds together] at the beginning and end of words. Words with /l/ /r/ /m/ and /n/ sounds such as pr-, fr-, kl-,kr-, thr-, - mp , -nt , -ps, and-ts etc. were very hard for Student A to segment from the other sounds in the words.

Reading Out Loud Samples:

Student A read two 3rd grade level stories for this sample. The first was read in its entirety two times.

We used the information on reading from Student A's December progress report for current reading level.

- Reading 2nd grade level text to 38 words per minute on 3 of 4 trials | Student A read mid-first grade text (Level H) to 26 words per minute per the progress report.

To see how Student A would read a grade level selection, the following samples were taken of Student A reading stories never seen before:

- Story #1 contained 253 words. Student A read it through in 6 minutes and 32 seconds on the first try [cold read]. Student A either needed help with decoding [interpreting the letters as words by coding sounds to the letters] or misread 19 words. That calculates to 39 words per minute at 93% accuracy.
- Story #2 was a one-minute cold read. Student A read 33 words with 76% accuracy.
  - o Errors included leaving out sounds and syllables in words.
  - o Strategies included sounding out one sound at a time for the one syllable words.
  - o Student A did not appear to be using syllable division or word endings as a strategy for decoding.
  - o Student A deleted [left out] the /r/ in blends and word endings.
  - o Student A added sounds or left out sounds to "make words" that were familiar but were not the words that were written. For example, Student A read the following: started for stared | tapped for trapped | comes for came | whole for wooden | powder for powdery
  - o Guessing appears to be Student A's main strategy.

STUDENT B

After collecting Student B's authentic writing, word spelling, sound play activities sample, and reading sample, Student B's reading, and spelling were mixed.

Student B was 7 years and 11 months old, and it was early in the first semester of second grade.

Authentic Writing: It was quite difficult to collect a writing sample from Student B because this student struggled to spell words. In fact, Student B worked so hard at getting letters down on the paper, that it was obvious when talking with this student that her ideas and speech were nothing like her writing.

Authentic Writing Sample 1: Words were spelled with 61.44% accuracy. A copy of the writing sample may be seen on the next page. Before Student B began to write, we talked about what she had done the past weekend and what might be included in the story about going to the Renaissance Festival. This prepared Student B to write.

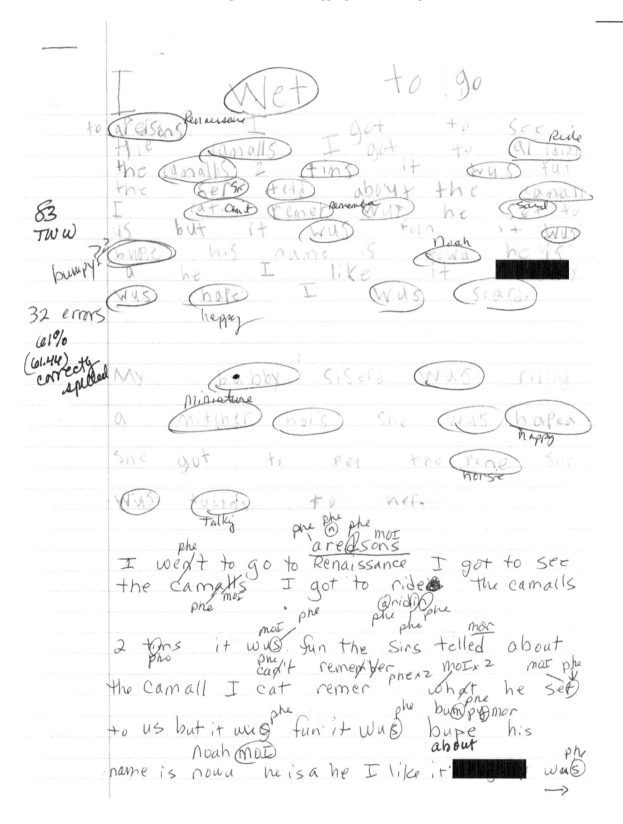

Word Level Spelling Sample: In the notes below C is used for Consonant and V is used for Vowel.

For example: A CVC word has a consonant , a vowel and then a consonant sound.

Word Spelling Sample List 1: CVC: 67%   Typical 3rd grade students spell 80% correctly.

Word Spelling Sample List 2: CCVC/CVCC/CCVCC: 40%

This list was not tested with classes of 2nd graders, but it was tested

with classes of 3rd graders and on average they spelled 80% correctly.

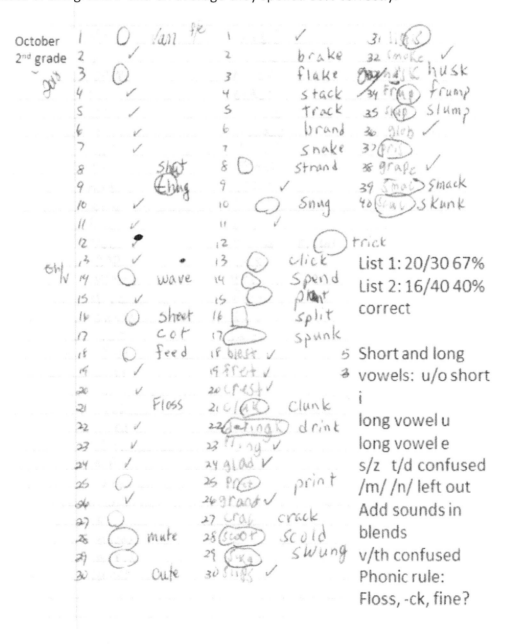

List 1: 20/30 67%

List 2: 16/40 40%

correct

Short and long

vowels: u/o short

i

long vowel u

long vowel e

s/z t/d confused

/m/ /n/ left out

Add sounds in

blends

v/th confused

Phonic rule:

Floss, -ck, fine?

9/15/18   [name]

		n/Deletion	
wet	went		nasal deletion
uredsons	renaissance	insertion x2	/n/d?
camalls	camels	MOI / Floss rule	
aridin	ride	insertion x 2	
tims	times	Phonics or	Long/short D.
wus	was	MOI	
sers	sirs	MOI	
teld	telled	floss + morph.	
cat	can't	nasal deletion	
remer	remember	Syll. D. /nasal + lateral D.	
wut	what	MOI	
set	sail	t/d /MOI	
buze (morph/nasal bumpy) or	about →	vowel dipthong (ou) p/t	
nowu	Noah	MOI	
hape	happy	phonic del/morph. or L/SH	
scard	scared	morph. -ed	
siserd	sister	insertion - d	
mitcher	miniature	Syll D.	
hors	horse	MOI	
hapen	happy	nasal insertion	
rone	horse	r/h n/s -/r	
toaing	talking	c-rule & MOI	
babby	baby	phonic - Dbl cons	

Sound Play Activity Samples

Parts of the [1] ABeCeDARIAN Placement Assessment was given to see if this student could name all the letters and their sounds and to read some of the stories to sample ability to read the words. No specified standard scores or criterion reference scores were used. I just wanted to hear Student B read and see if Student B knew the letter sounds.

Please note that when you see a letter between two / / [forward slash] marks, that stands for the sound of that letter. When the letter is written between [apostrophes] ' ' that stands for the name of the letter.

Student B knew all the letter sounds except /y/, which was read as a short /u/ sound. Student B struggled so much with blending and segmenting sounds in words that this student was not testable.

Reading Sample: We met twice to collect Student B's samples. Since Student B was struggling to read the words on any page, I tried giving a few opportunities to read silently and to practice reading the passage twice before timing to see if reading would improve. Doing this provides a chance to see if reading out loud is affecting reading rate and accuracy. In Student B's case, reading fluency improved when given an opportunity to read over the material as a preview. The reading sample information about when the child reads faster or more accurately will be useful to other teachers working with the student as well.

Cold Read	Kindergarten Level	28 wpm, 73% accuracy
Repeated read 3x--	Kindergarten Level	28 wpm, 73% accuracy
Cold Read	2nd grade level	25 wpm, 80% accuracy
		[one month later-no lessons yet]
After Silent Read:	1st grade Level	57 wpm, 93% accuracy
After Silent Read:	2nd grade level	26 wpm, 88% accuracy
Repeated read 3x--	2nd grade level	54 wpm, 93% accuracy

Student B is an example of a child with an especially severe case of difficulty matching sounds to letters, blending sounds, and segmenting the sounds in words. Sounds that are voiced [/th/ as in "them" were easier than sounds that are not ['think']. Student B confused /f/ and the /th/ sound [think] which is not voiced and did not process the /m/ , /n/ , /r/ or /l/ sounds. All the short vowels sounded the same, so matching short vowels to letters was extremely hard.

Student B was new to the school district she now attended and was reading and writing at a preschool level at the beginning of second grade. No information regarding previous teaching methods nor interventions was available. The new school did indicate that Student B was reading at Level C on the Fountas and Pinnell reading assessment. Level C is what might be expected of a child entering kindergarten.

I would like to take a minute, at this point, to speak directly to parents and especially parents who home school their children.

The system presented here is not rocket science. It is entirely possible to look closely at what a child does when reading and spelling to learn a great deal about what they do not understand. Educators often use fancy, $5 words [yes, I plead guilty to doing this], but it is not necessary to use words people may not understand to talk about what you see your child doing with words, sounds and letters when they read and spell. So, parents collect the samples, look at what is there, and look for patterns of mistakes. You are just as capable of doing this as any teacher or SLP [Speech Language Pathologist].

[1] The ABeCeDARIAN Placement Assessment may be obtained in PDF at https://www.pathstoliteracy.org/resources/abecedarian-reading-assessment

STUDENT C

I first met with Student C in 2nd grade. Student C's reading was grade level at that time, so no further services were provided. Then in 3rd grade new concerns emerged regarding written language, so we took a second look. As it turned out, Student C was reading 82 words per minute on 3rd grade reading material with only 2 errors. Student C was able to verbally answer questions about what was read; however, Student C could not write answers to questions, due to multiple spelling errors. Student C was very selective about which words to write and avoided words student C could not spell. While reading remained a little slow, this was related more to lack of opportunity to practice. Student C needed repeated reading.

Many schools use the Fountas and Pinnell system for measuring reading skills. When measurements are taken, responses are given verbally so spelling disabilities would not be noticed. However, when Student C was asked to respond to questions in writing across all subject areas, it was a problem. Math story problems were especially problematic for this reason.

Authentic writing Sample: Student C spelled 21 of 41 words correctly for 51% spelling accuracy.

Word Spelling Sample List 1: CVC: 22/30 73%   Typical 3rd grade students spell 80% correctly.

Word Spelling Sample List 2: CCVC/CVCC/CCVCC: 33/40 82%

List 3 was not given due to time constraints, as I visited Student C's classroom to collect the sample.

Student C presented with low average skills for reading and spelling, but since Student C's parents were concerned, Student C began receiving 20 Minute Phonemic Training intervention once a week over the span of three months. Student C was in a structured classroom where the teacher was presenting phonics rules for reading and spelling daily and following up to confirm understanding.

Student C had difficulty with segmenting sounds in the Sound Activity samples and was not matching [sometimes referred to as mapping] sounds to all the letters correctly. When writing, Student C struggled with switching sounds and letters around in words, leaving sounds out, inserting some sounds incorrectly and mixing up some letters and sounds. This student also needed to work on phonics for the final e rule. Specific letters and sounds we addressed were b/d reversals, 'x', 'ch', 'n', 'z', and the long /u/ sounds. Student C was also confused about when to use the letter 'k' or the letter 'c' at the beginning of a word.

At this point we now have specific sounds, letters, and phonemic awareness skills that we know are strengths and weaknesses for our students.

We are ready for Step 2.

CHAPTER 3

STEP 2: Four Steps to organize for the lessons

First: Turn the numbers in your spelling samples into percentages.
Authentic Writing Sample:

1. Count how many words were written. Count every word, including 'a', 'and,' 'the' etc.   For example, let us say that 100 words were written.
2. Count how many words were misspelled. For example, let us say that 30 words were misspelled
3. Next find the percentage of words that were spelled correctly.

The reason we do this is to decide whether the student is making progress when we are checking progress later. In 2009 writing samples from two classrooms of fifth grade students were reviewed, 45 students in all. On average, the students spelled 91.6% of the words they wrote correctly, the mode was 100%, and the median was 95%.
Here is an example of how the average percentage of correctly spelled words is found.

1. 100 words counted.
2. 30 mistakes found.
3. 100 take away 30 words misspelled equals 70 words spelled correctly. 100-30=70
4. Divide 70 mistakes by 100 words and that equals .70.
5. Move the decimal point over two spaces to the right and add a percent sign [%].
There are 70% correctly spelled words.

Word Level Spelling Sample: Find the percentage of correctly spelled words on each list given.

Example: List 1:

1. There are 30 words.
2. There were 15 mistakes.
3. 30 take away 15 mistakes equals 15 words spelled correctly. 30 – 15 = 15
4. Divide 15 mistakes by 30 words and that equals .50.
5. Move the decimal point over two spaces to the right and add a percent sign [%].
There are 50% correctly spelled words.

Second: *Playing with Sounds Sample*: Find the percentage of correctly answered tasks. You will have six percentages or one for each kind of task.

1. Count how many words were given in each group [blending, segmenting, taking sounds away, adding sounds, changing sounds, and switching sounds around.
2. Count how many tasks in each group were performed correctly.

Use the following example as your guide.   Example for Blending:

1. You gave the student 10 words.
2. They missed 4 words.
3. 10-4=6 words blended correctly.
4. 6 words blended correctly divided by 10 words given = .60
5. 60% of the words were correctly blended.

Do this same calculation for each task.

- Segmenting, leaving one sound out,
- Inserting, adding one sound,
- Substituting, changing one sound
- Reversing, switching two sounds around.

Sometimes a child is not testable for one or more sections of this test. When students miss five words on any one of these tasks, stop testing and note that they were not testable for this skill and that you will practice this skill with them.

Third: *Reading Fluency Sample*: [how FAST and how ACCURATELY] the student can read is calculated.

We will do the same type of calculation for the reading sample, but we will also need to know how fast the student read. Please refer to the ***Fluency Calculator*** in Chapter 11 for detailed instructions.

Fourth: Write all the numbers and percentages on the Summary Sheet. See example below.

SUMMARY PAGE

Name: Sierra	Date:	Date:	Date:
	18-Jan	18-May	
Authentic Writing	76% & 77%	91% & 97%	
Word List 1	76%	87%	
Word List 2	65%	80%	
Word List 3	na	na	
Blending CVC	not automatic	100%	
Blending CCVC-CVCC	not automatic	100%	
Segmenting CVC	80%+	100%	
Segmenting CCVC-CVCC	80%+	100%	
Deleting CVC	<80%	90%	
Deleting CCVC-CVCC	<80%	90%	

Use the Summary Sheet to describe and summarize the kinds of spelling, reading, and sound errors the student made. There could be more than one kind of error in one mistake.
For example,

If the student reads or writes the word 'black' as 'back,' then there is a

- Deletion {left out the /l/ when reading black [back]}

If the student reads or writes the word 'black' as 'bulack,' then there is an

- Insertion {added the short vowel /u/ between the first two letters [bulak]

If the student writes the word 'black' as 'bak,' then the

- Phonic rule for -ck is not understood {used only the letter 'a' when spelling [blak]}

The information you just collected will be used to

1. Compare how your child is growing over the next few months.
2. Select word lists that you will use for your mini lessons.
3. Decide which sound play skills you will use for practice in your mini lessons.

To help you see how your notes will be organized, a copy of Student A's reading and writing scores can be found on the next page with scores from before and after working through lessons over three months.

Describe the Mistakes | Describe what you See

Summary Page

Name: Sierra	Date:	Date:	Date:
	18-Jan	18-May	
Authentic Writing	76% & 77%	91% & 97%	
Word List 1	76%	87%	
Word List 2	65%	80%	
Word List 3	no	no	
Blending CVC	not automatic	100%	
Blending CCVC-CVCC	not automatic	100%	
Segmenting CVC	80%+	100%	
Segmenting CCVC-CVCC	80%+	100%	
Deleting CVC	<80%	90%	
Deleting CCVC-CVCC	<80%	90%	
Inserting CVC	<80%	90%	
Inserting CCVC-CVCC	<80%	90%	
Substituting CVC	<80%	90%	
Substituting CCVC-CVCC	<80%	90%	
Reverse CVC	not testable	90%	
Reverse CVC-CVCC	not testable	90%	
Discriminating between voiced & voiceless sounds	<80%	100%	
Discriminating between short vowel tones	<80%	100%	
Reading Selection Level	1st grade	3rd	
Reading Accuracy	unknown	unknown	
Reading Rate--Words Per Minute	26 wpm	42 wpm	
Reading Selection Level	2nd grade		
Reading Accuracy	unknown		
Reading Rate--Words Per Minute	38 wpm		
Reading Selection Level	3rd grade	3rd grade	
Reading Accuracy	76%	96%	
Reading Rate--Words Per Minute	40 wpm	81 wpm	
Reading errors deletions:			
Reading errors inserting:			
Reading errors substituting:			
Sound and letter errors: pre		b/d | f/th | all short vowels t f th k p s sh m n ng	
Sound and letter errors: post		none	
phonic rules: pre		FlOSS final e -ck -dge	
PHONIC RULES: post		only a few -ck -dge errors remain	

How to Describe Kinds of Spelling or Reading Errors

There are 5 KINDS of mistakes a student might make. A reference list for the kinds of spelling errors is found in Chapter 11. The five kinds of mistakes made are:

Sound or Phonemic mistake

1) Does the child not hear each sound in the word correctly? Maybe sounds run together so only part of the sounds are read or represented with letters when they try to write the words. Phonemic errors [missing sounds, misrepresented sounds, or sounds out of sequence]. [See Chapter 11 for more on this type of error]. For example:

a. Spelling ' fed' for 'Fred' or 'thread' or 'third' | /r/ is omitted |
b. /f/ is substituted for the /th/ sound in thread and third
c. Writing 'sall' for 'saw' |or final phoneme /aw/ is written as /awl/
d. Writing 'theek' or 'theke' for 'think' | nasal /n/ left out| /i/ is interpreted as a long /e/
e. We will review more on this type of mistake later in the Chapter.

Phonic Rule errors

2) Phonic rule errors involve specific letter patterns that occur with various other letters or vowel tones. Phonic rules tell us how letters can line up in words and rely on what you hear. For example, short vowel sounds are tied to the -ck rule, a letter sequence that only appears after short vowels.

Phonic rules are taught in the first two or three grades of school. This creates a problem for struggling readers. Since you need to have 'sound' skills [phonemic processing] before phonic rules 'make sense', teaching the rules before students have good auditory skills may confuse them.

Spelling may also be a frustration because, to spell correctly students need to:

a. 'hear' the differences between vowel tones and voiced / voiceless sounds [discrimination skills].
b. 'hear' sounds separately and combine them into meaningful words [phonemic blending]. Teachers and parents tell students to 'sound out the word.' This is fine — IF you can put the sounds together!
c. separate the sounds [segmentation]. Again, when students are writing unknown words, separating sounds [sounding the words out] helps them assign letters to the sounds. This only works if they 'hear' all the sounds in the word and CAN separate them.
d. 'hear' the vowel tone and remember to add the final 'e' after a CVC word to make the vowel long.

Coping strategies children use and reasons for phonic errors:
1. Children try to remember the letter sequence for the words [visual memory].
2. They do not say the sounds, so they do not know if the vowel needs a final 'e' or not.
3. Another error happens with –ck, because students are not sure where it goes! For example: ' like' might be spelled 'licke' I often see this occur after the teacher presents a lesson on the –ck rule. Another example would be 'lik.' In this case the rule may not be known.
4. The student does not:
   a. understand/know the rule or
   b. hear the difference between the long and short vowel tones – which takes us back to a phonemic error or
   c. is not saying the sounds as he/she writes the words to cue him/her what to write.
   d. See Chapter 11 for a list comparing long and short vowel phonic rules compared side by side.

Morphological errors

3) Morphological errors are related to the grammar of the English language. We add endings to words to indicate 'how many' [plural endings] or 'when' [verb tenses], etc.
   a. Examples of word ending mistakes: [Morphological] Do they leave the ending /s/ off verbs?[He puts his hat on when he goes outside.] Do they leave off the ending -ed when something already happened? [The boy jumped off his bike.] They may not understand the need to show 'already happened' with the -ed marker. If you find that they used the wrong letter [maybe a /t/ sound], then it could be that they understand the rule, but do not understand how to spell the ending; OR they do not hear the sound correctly.
   b. The brain fires neurons in response to sounds. Brain imaging of the Broca's area of the brain shows how much time the brain needs to perceive the sounds. The brain is working hard to 'hear' the rapid sound signals it receives. The immature brain of a child is learning to separate sentences, syllables, words, and phonemes into smaller units. Sounds overlap and the brain must learn to separate them.
      - A vowel sound lasts 100-150 milliseconds.
      - A one syllable word [look] 200 milliseconds.
      - Add a suffix [looks or looked] and time increases to 320 milliseconds
      - Create a complete grammatical phrase [I am looking] and the time increases to 450 milliseconds.[1]

----

[1]Sahin, N., Pinker, S., Cash, S., Schomer, D., and Halgren, E. (2009) of Lexical, Sequential Processing, Grammatical, and Phonological Information within Broca's Area. Science, 326, 444-44

c. Toddlers, preschoolers, and children hear words with various endings in daily conversation thousands of times. Their brains create patterns for language based upon hearing the same language patterns over and over. The brain cannot form the 'patterns of rules' for language when it does not hear the same pattern repeatedly. This happens when they have middle ear fluid or ear infections. This also happens when they are constantly hearing language with a lot of background noise drowning out the speech signal at the same time. High frequency sounds are especially vulnerable to background noise.

Meaning mistake [Semantic]

4) Word meanings must be understood to know which spelling to choose. [SEM] Semantic errors are related more to vocabulary development than phonemic. We have many words that sound the same but are spelled differently.

- For example: writing   hour for our, 'Hare' is a rabbit, 'hair' grows on your head.
- 'There' is a place and 'their' is a pronoun showing ownership.

Remember How to Spell It: [Mental Orthographic Imagery or MOI]

5) There are some words that defy sound, phonic and word ending patterns. We simply must remember how those words are spelled. About 20% of the words we use fall into this category.

- For example, *nife* for *knife* or *lite* for *light* or *wen* for *when* have spellings that depart from what we expect.

More about Phonemic or Sound Errors

Phonemic errors are the most common type that we see, and Phonic rule errors come in second. When sounds are not distinguished and/or correctly matched to letters, phonic rules do not make sense, because phonic rules are dependent upon what is heard. Therefore, we want to know what the student is thinking when they 'hear' sounds in words so we can know what to teach each student. In Chapter 11 **you can see *a list of phonic rules with examples.*** The phonic rule cards in Chapter 11 may be photocopied, laminated, and turned into a card set to display for the student to use as a reference.

Here are the kinds of reading and spelling errors that might be made when processing sounds:

1. *Vowel Discrimination or Mix up vowel sounds.* – Sometimes called a "Discrimination error" This causes the child to be unable to tell one vowel sound from another.

   a. There are 6 short vowel tones, and those tones follow the position of your jaw from closed to open. With your teeth together and tongue high, we say /i/. Open slightly to say /e/. Open a bit more to say /a/, next /u/ and finally the jaw is open for /o/. The problem seems to be that approximately 20% to 30% of people do not 'hear' or 'process' the fine tonal changes between the short vowel tones [discriminate between them]. Plus, others even have difficulty processing the difference between long and short vowel tones.

   b. In first and second grade teachers teach how to read and write words with short and long vowels along with the phonic rules associated with them. Double letter vowels are also introduced and may cause confusion if discrimination between tones is not established.

   c. Did you know that the human mind, on average, can only hold 6 sounds at a time for comparison? This holds true for comparing almost anything. Malcolm Gladwell in the book "Tipping Point" discusses this phenomena and notes that we can only hold 6 flavors or 6 smells in our minds at a time and tell them apart for comparing. It seems that when more are added, the brain cannot hold more than six in memory to be able to accurately compare. This phenomenon is called "channel capacity" in cognitive psychology. [1]

   d. Leave sounds out. —Sometimes called "deletion." Deleting sounds usually happens when there are two consonants together at the beginning or end of a word.

2. *Reversals* switch the order of the sound. For example, the word "crab" might be spelled "carb" or "turn" might be spelled "trun."

----

[1] Gladwell, Malcolm. Tipping Point, publ. Little, Brown, and Company, copyright 2000 and 2002, page 175-176.

3. *Sound substitutions* are like discrimination errors. In this situation the child will consistently [or almost consistently] write a different letter for a sound. They may always use the letter 'f' for 'v' or "g" for 'j,' for example. Whenever you see a sound substitution, then you are also seeing discrimination, or the child has learned to associate sounds to letters incorrectly. When children use sound substitutions in their speech as toddlers, even once this is corrected, it sometimes remains in their writing. Some examples of substitutions are:

  a. /k/, /g/ or /t/ may be substituted for each other
  b. /p/, /b/ may be mixed up
  c. /t/ /d/ may be mixed up
  d. /f/ /v/ or /th/ maybe be substituted for each other
  e. /s/ /z/ or /sh/ may be substituted for each other
  f. /sh/ /ch/ may be mixed up
  g. /w/ may be used for /r/ or /l/
  h. /g/ maybe written for /j/ as in /judge/
  i. /m/ /n/ may be confused

More about Phonic Rule Errors

The word test will be the best place for reviewing Phonic Rule Errors, [refer to results from Chapter 1], but their reading and writing samples may also reveal some information. The following rules are included in the word level assessment.

- FLOSS
- -ck
- -tch
- -dge
- Doubling consonants
- -final e rule with open and closed syllables
- -le syllable

When children make a lot of phonic rule errors and they have phonemic [or sound errors too], this might mean that phonic rules do not make sense since the student does not "process" the sounds.

- Rules about letter patterns and sounds are meaningless to them because they are missing half of the information needed to apply the phonic rules.
- On the other hand, when children have few phonemic errors, then the phonic rules may need to be taught with the sound relationship in mind.

CHAPTER 4

STEP 3: Set Up the Lessons

We now have a 'picture' of your students' reading skills, spelling ability and error patterns we can use to 'fill in' the missing pieces in their skills when we present the lessons. So now it is time to look at your Summary Chart. Here you will see which sounds or combinations of sounds to include in the lessons:

In Chapters 6 and 7 there are 160 lists. There are 10 lists of chained words with 10 words in each list per page. For each group of letters shown at the top of a page, you will have 10 chains of 10 words, or 100 words for each set of sounds and group of letters. Each of the sets has a teacher page [the first page], a word reading page for the student to read and check their own spelling at the end of the lesson [the second page], and a sentence page for each list [10 sentences] for the student to read or to use for dictation and spelling in context of a sentence [the third page]. This pattern repeats 3 to 4 times for each kind of syllable. You will select one list for each 20-minute lesson.

In STEP 3, refer to the headings on the lists and select pages and list numbers to use for your child based upon the sounds and letters missed when they were writing and reading. Your summary sheet has all this information.

Make a list of each page and list number for reference and check them off as your student completes a lesson for each set of words. This completes your planning for all or most of your lessons before you even begin! As you progress through the lessons, you may find your student no longer has difficulty with a given sound and be able to skip some lists that you have marked. That is fine. Adjust to your students' needs.

Select the size of the syllable to use in the lessons using the following guidelines

If your student had trouble with …

- short vowel tones [ex. 'sit' for 'set' | 'lag' for 'leg' | 'log' for 'lug']
- mixing short and long vowel tones [ex. 'lik' for 'like' | 'sun' for 'soon']
- leaving off final e for long vowel tones [ex. 'lik' for 'like' | 'sam' for 'same']
- observing the phonic rules for FLOSS, -ck, -tch or -dge [ex. 'sik' / 'sick' | 'cach' / 'catch'| 'fuj' / 'fudge'
- mixing up /sh/ and /ch/ [ex. 'shoo' for 'chew' |'chin' / 'shin' |'wish' /'which'
- confusing /f/ and /th/ { ex. 'baf' / 'bath' | 'wif' /'with' | 'fing' / 'thing'
- confusing /n/ /m/ and /ng/ [ex. 'fin' /thing/ | /'fun'/ 'thumb'
- mixing up /b/ with /p/ or /d/ [ex. 'rod' for 'rot |'rod' for rob] | "das' / 'bass' | 'dos' / boss'
- confusing voiced and voiceless sounds: /t/ /d/ /p/ /b/ /k/ /g/ /f/ /v/ /s/ /z/ ['tot'/dot |'pat'/bat'| 'pad/bat | kik /gig | fif/five |'fis' /'fizz']

...then you will begin with CVC word lists, begin with Chapter 6

Scores below 80% spelling accuracy and 95% reading accuracy for Sound Play on CVC words are good indications that you will start with Chapter 6. Also, when there are a lot of phonic rule errors, begin with this Chapter. The letters and sounds for each list are written at the top of each page of lists. Select lists with the same letters and sounds you have listed as errors on the summary page.

If your child scored 80% or higher on List 1 Word Level spelling test AND did not show many phonic rule errors, CVC word misspelling OR miss words in their authentic writing or when reading, then you will begin with words from the lists in Chapter 7.

If this is where you are beginning, then your student likely will have made mistakes,

- leaving sounds out of beginning or ending blends [ex. 'sop'/ 'top'/stop | 'gup'/jump | 'bik'or 'bike'/'blink']
- adding sounds separating sounds in blends [ex. 'felat'/'flat' |' berak'/'break '| 'buled'/ 'blend']
- adding an extra sound to the end of a word [ex. 'runa'/ 'run | 'gupa' or 'jumpa / 'jump']
- switching sounds around within a word having blends [ex. 'crab'/' carb'|'trun'/'turn']
- reading and writing words with /n/, /m/ and /ng/ sounds [-mp, -nd, -nk, -nt, etc.] [ex. 'jug'/ 'jump' | 'rik' or 'ring'/'rink' | 'sed'/'send']

If your child scored well on lists 1 and 2, did not have difficulty with most phonic rules, spelled short vowel and long vowel tones correctly [for final e rule, not necessarily vowel digraphs], then begin with Chapter 8. Here you want to review the rule for doubling consonants and the kinds of syllables there are. Be sure to take time to review and practice the rule for spelling two-syllable words if your student scored below 85% on List 3. As you look at your students' writing take note of errors like the examples below:

- when spelling words ending with -le [ex. 'tabil' / 'tabl' for 'table'| hudl /for huddle]
- adding the past tense -ed ending [ex. 'rapt' / wrapped | 'pod' / potted]
- spelling or reading words ending with plurals [-es after /ch/ and /sh/, -ts, -ps, ['lit' or 'list' for 'lists' | 'get' / 'gets' | 'push' or pushs for 'pushes' |' catchs' or cachz for 'catches'
- adding verb ending 's' and 'ing' [ex 'get' /'gets' | 'push' /' pushes' | rubing / rubbing

....then use Chapter 8-word lists.

The final step will be learning about multiple syllable words, suffixes, and the unstressed/stressed syllable. Chapter 9 covers how to do this in detail with worksheets.

After you decide which syllable level you will use to begin, then go to the lists in Chapters 6,7, and/or 8. Select lists for the sounds and letters you have noted on your summary page, write the page and list numbers for each word chain list that addresses the mistakes your student made [refer to your summary page.] Chapters 6 and 7 contain lists of words grouped by kinds of sounds and length of syllables. Select the lists matching those sounds or sound patterns your student missed when reading and spelling.

For the higher level student, for each lesson you will select 5 or 10 two-syllable words from the lists in chapter 8. This is when you will discuss topics such as: when and why we use -ing, -ed, -er or -est, etc. You will explore changing words by adding the common grammatical endings related to quality or time.

Phonemic Skills: Blending ,Discrimination [between short vowel tones, long/short vowel tones, segmenting, deleting, and substituting sounds]

Phonic rules: FLOSS final e for long vowels   -ck   -dge

Letters and Sounds: f/th   k   p   s/sh   m/n/ng

Lower case b and d

Repeated reading practice with phrasing exercises.

Page	List #	Page	List #	Page	List#	Page	List#
40	3,4						
41	3,4						
42	3,4						
43	12,13,16						
44	12,13,16						
45	2,3,6						
49	31,32,33,34,35,37						
50	31,32,33,34,35,37						
51	1,2,3,4,5,7						
52	2,3						
53	2,3						
54	2,3						
55	17,19,20						
56	17,19,20						
57	7,9,10						
58	23,24,25,26,28						
59	23,24,25,26,28						
60	3,4,5,6,8						
61	all						
62	all						
63	all						
64	3a,4,6,7,9						
66	all						
67	all						
70	3a,4,6,7,9						
71	3a,4,6,7,9						
72	3a,4,6,7,9						
Etc.							

One of my favorite days to work with the students, besides the day we complete the training, is the first day. It seems like the first day we work together is when they begin to realize that someone understands their frustrations, believes in them and that something different is about to begin.

Keep in mind that we are starting out with children or adults who have struggled for a while, maybe even years, have begun to doubt whether they will ever be like the other kids, and they are thinking they may never 'get' how to read and spell. The first lesson day is when we introduce hope that all is about to change.

To 'set the table' tell them the following story. Please understand we are not trying to be literally, historically correct. Instead, give them a basis for what we are about to begin.

At this point, I begin to make each sound in their name while reaching out into the air as if grasping it and setting it into position from their left to right before their face. "[/t/ - /o/ - /m/ /ee/]." If you are across from them, be sure you are doing this from THEIR left to THEIR right!

"There. Could you see those sounds? Can you see your name up there? Of course not! We cannot see sounds! But sounds are all around us. We just cannot see them. We hear them. I imagine that a very long time ago, when the first people were learning to talk to each other, they had a problem. They did not have cars, radio, or telephones. When they wanted to tell you something, they had to SEE you. They could not even mail a letter! They also did NOT have books or letters to write words! So, they drew pictures, but they did not have paper either. They drew on the walls of their homes, in the dirt, or on rocks. They drew pictures of people, trees, and animals. They had one BIG problem. Some words they used could not be drawn, because they could not be seen. If they wanted to tell you that something was 'easy' to do, they could not draw a picture of 'easy'. Then someone figured out that there are sounds inside each word -- /ee/-/z/- /ee/. They made up 'pictures' for each /sound/ used in words, and letters were born. In our language there are only forty-four of sounds we use to make words, but we can make thousands of words by mixing up and adding sounds together to make lots of words."

"Letters are pictures of sounds. Now all they had to do was draw the 'picture, or letter' for each sound in a word and then someone else could look at the sound pictures, connect them together and say the word. Time passed. People were scattered all over the world. People started making rules about how to draw the sound pictures and which letters could sit next to other letters and different ways to spell words. That is how reading and writing words began."

Together, we are going to play with sounds and match them to the 'pictures.' We are going to be taking the sounds apart and putting them together until it is easy for you to read and write words.

"You learned to talk all by yourself. You connected many sounds to say many words when you were very little. Words are made of lots of sounds that are connected together."

A video example of the story "Letters are Pictures of Sounds" may be viewed at https://youtu.be/cqxcGaRv9yg
A video example of how to demonstrate the difference between a vowel and consonant sound may be viewed at https://youtu.be/sp5bAlD9Dak

CHAPTER 5

STEP 4: The 20 Minute Lesson

The lesson includes 4 parts from beginning to end.

This is the step where you will need most of the materials listed at the beginning of Chapter 1 and your first word list. Refer to Chapter 1 and gather your materials before you begin the lesson.

Part A: Blending.

Begin by speaking each of the sounds within the first word on the list one sound at a time [you are segmenting]. Ask the student to tell you the word [the student is blending the phonemes]. Nearly all are real words but may be unknown to the student. Talk about word meanings when this arises. Occasionally nonsense words are included. When a list contains a nonsense word, I challenge them to find the nonsense word in today's list. Use this as an opportunity to teach recognition of errors in decoding or spelling by noting that a word does not make sense. ***This should take approximately 3 to 5 minutes.*** Record students' scores on the student worksheet or your logging sheet.

Four Strategies for Blending When Students Struggle

Model: Use marbles that are flat on one side. Slide them together as you connect the sounds. Use the phrase 'voice on' or 'sing' the sounds. Give student marbles to repeat.

1. Model: Place flat marbles of 5 different colors before the student. Each marble represents one SOUND. Leave spaces between each marble. Touch each one as you speak each sound [segmented] in the word, then push the marbles together and speak the syllable with sounds blended. Next, have the student 'blend' [push together] the marbles and say sounds. No marbles? Try square pieces of paper or coins.

2. Model: Make a dot for each sound on a paper. Then use a crayon and with 'voice on', draw a flowing line as you connect the dots [sounds]. Give your student crayon and paper to repeat.

3. Model: Stroke your arm, voice on, as you connect the sounds. Ask them to repeat.

4. Place paper shapes on the floor in a sequence [for example: circle, triangle, square = pat; or circle, triangle, circle = pop] and step on each one while speaking a phoneme for a word. Next, ask the student to repeat the sequence / movement and then sing or say the word.

Part B: SEGMENTING and AUDITORY TRACKING [for DISCRIMINATION or telling the difference between sounds that are similar].

Give the student the worksheet [circle & triangle page] with something to use for marking the circles [stickers, ink stamper, marker, OR paint dauber]. Say each word one at a time, and ask the student to repeat the word, while saying each sound in the word [segmenting] and marking a shape for each sound [phoneme] in the syllable. [See list of materials needed at the beginning of Chapter 1] {Hint: Paint Daubers are the fastest tool}. For each syllable after the first one, they will only mark a circle for the 'different' phoneme from the PREVIOUS word. This exercise requires them to segment, remember, sequence, and compare the sounds in both syllables. At first, they will have trouble doing this. Model the activity by pointing to each shape and segmenting the sounds in chorus with the student. Then ask questions for each sound comparison to help them learn how to compare the sounds. ***This should take approximately 10 to 13 minutes.*** **For virtual instruction, we use annotate or screen share giving student control to draw or highlight the shapes.**

For example, using the words "pit & pet" - prompt "Tell me the sounds in pit." "Tell me the sounds in pet." "Which sound is different in the second word?"

If they cannot find the different sound or choose the wrong sound say:

> "Tell me the first sound in pit and the first sound in pet." [pointing to the paper shapes]   "Are the sounds the same or different? "
>
> "What do you feel when you say ____ ["p"] sound?" "What part of your mouth moves?" "tongue?" "lips?" "jaw?"
>
> Say /i/. Then ask, "Does /i/ match the first sound in "is" or "Eddy"?
>
> Say /e/. Then ask, "Does /e/ match the first sound in "is" or "Eddy"

Practice the mnemonic[1] sentence: "Is Eddy At Uncle Ollie's?" Say "/i/ - 'is' Does the first sound in 'is' match /i/, or does /i/ match "Eddy?" Do this for each phoneme in the sequence until they arrive at the correct sound change.

Sometimes they will not get it. When this occurs, model with a mirror and repeat the two sounds while explaining the difference in movement. Use questions like, "What part of your mouth is moving?" or "Does your jaw go up or down when you say /i/ then /e/?"

Continue through the list until all 10 syllables are completed. Record the score.

At CVC level sound deletions are not a significant activity, however it is a valuable skill when learning to segment and spell words containing initial and final blends. For example, when one sound is removed the following words may be created: pat/at; slip/lip; slip/sip, etc. Most lists will have at least two or three words that you can play with by taking one sound away to create a new word. Take a few seconds to show this to your student in preparation for more difficult lists later.

Reversals: A CCV worksheet is included for beginning blends.   A separate page is included at the beginning of Chapter 8 for practicing sound reversals. Sound reversals often present in student writing when students have trouble sequencing sounds. Teaching them deliberate sound reversing is helpful when addressing sequencing issues. For example, pit/tip, tap/pat; bat/tab; flit/felt; or trim/term.

----

[1] **Mnemonic is a pattern of letters or associations that assists in remembering something**
Strategies for Tracking and Segmenting Sound Changes Between Syllables

When Students Struggle

1. Say the syllable aloud first. Talk about movement. Every mouth movement creates a new sound. Practice with letter names. The letter 'B' or' b' name is two movements and two sounds /b/ +/e/. Many of the consonant letter names contain their sound, but also have another sound connected to them. B, D, J, K, P, Q, T, V, Z all have their sound at the beginning of their names. F, L, M, N, R, S have their sound at the end of the letter name and X, C, G, H, W, Y say sounds that are different from their letter names.
2. Next, touch each shape as you speak each sound. Stop your voice between sounds.
3. Cue them to compare each jaw or tongue movement between words.
   - Touch the next row of shapes and say the new word.
   - Touch the previous row and repeat that word.
   - Have the student repeat both words and touch/speak the sounds in each word to compare the two and find the 'change' in the second word.
4. Be ready to say the sound with the student until they can remember and segment on their own.
5. If the student cannot remember the previous syllable for comparison: Tell them: Listen to yourself and think about how your mouth, tongue and lips are moving for each sound. Then think about how your mouth, tongue and lips are moving in the second word.

Watch video demonstrations of strategies here: video:
Video: https://youtu.be/H_HFX2izaaY

Part C: The reading exercise is the application of skills practiced.

The previous exercises address the common core objectives for phonological and phonemic awareness. Awareness and ability to manipulate sounds in words is foundational to decoding.[1] When students are decoding unknown words, remind them to think about matching sounds with letters.

Say: "Be sure to blend the sounds. Keep your voice turned on." If difficulties persist, have them begin with the last sound and add one sound at a time until all sounds are blended; this is sometimes called 'backward chaining.' Reading the words and sentences should take about 3 to 5 minutes.

Another strategy is to speak the initial and final blends as units and 'sing' the sounds together, until they reach automaticity with the mapping and blending of phonemes to letters as they read.

In addition to reading the sentences provided, the student should be reading short fluency passages containing primarily sight words at the kindergarten and first grade level with CVC words for those students working with CVC words. Five passages that are leveled with the Frye Readability Scale are included in Chapter 11.

A break from the exercises to repeatedly read a passage three times in a row for one minute each time, is a tangible demonstration to the student of their own progress and highly motivational. Having the student chart the number of words read, and the number of errors made provides them with visual proof of their learning progress. When parents support this activity by doing it with their children three times a week, progress is even more impressive.[2]

When students are consistently successful with any of the individual skills [blending, segmenting, tracking], skip those exercises. Note: some sight words are included in the sentences. Sight words are normally part of the classroom reading instruction and are important in the development of reading, although not useful as the ONLY tool in the development of reading and writing skills.

Sometimes the student can lift the words from the page, but their reading is very choppy. In these cases, phrasing is usually the issue. They may be breathing too frequently or not breathing in the right places. Choral reading and modeling phrasing can help. You can mark the space between phrases where the student will breathe, then read the selection with phrasing to them, next read the passage in chorus followed by the student reading it alone. After a few passages practiced in this manner, the student is usually ready to try it on their own and will do very well.

[1]DeHaene, Stanislas, "READING IN THE BRAIN" Copyright © 2009 by Stanislas Dehaene. This book is available in eBook or paperback on Amazon.com

[2]Dowhower, Sarah L. "Repeated reading: Research into practice" This article reports on the benefits of repeated reading, various ways to conduct repeated reading exercises, and classroom applications of repeated reading.

Part D: Finally, read the syllables for the student to write,
[like a spelling test]. When writing, have them use the sentence "Is Eddy At Uncle Ollie's" for comparing the vowel tones to letters to aid correct mapping of short vowel tones to letters, if they struggle with the vowel sounds. [I post the picture of Eddy at his Uncle Ollie's home on a wall nearby as a reminder to the student to use the mnemonic tool for discrimination between short vowel tones. See Chapter 11.] Record the number of words correctly spelled. This should take approximately 3 to 5 minutes.

Writing and spelling require ability to recognize phonemes and map them to letters when writing. The writing exercise is the application of skills practiced. Some useful strategies include: Remind them to say each sound in the syllable as they write it.
Tell them:

- Match the sounds to the letters.
- Use your mouth movements to help you match the sounds and letters.[1]
- Give them water and a paintbrush and ask them to say each sound while painting the corresponding letters or letter combinations to spell words.
- Practice skywriting. Model the spelling by writing it with your finger in the air and ask them to tell you the sequence of letters used by stating each sound rather than the letter names. This may become a blending task as well if only phonemes are presented, and they must blend the phonemes as well as identify and map the letters to sounds. This exercise helps to develop visual with auditory memory while using large muscle movement. Writing on the tabletop with fingers is another variation on this activity.
  - One note of caution: Be sure the student 'sees' the movement [letters] from left to right. If you are sitting across from the student, you will need to write backwards from right to left!

When proficient in the use of mouthing and segmenting sounds as they write and spell words on the lists to eighty percent accuracy, give them the dictated sentence from the "sentence reading list" for the word set the student is studying. Students respond well t0o immediate feedback when writing words and sentences, so give them a score for each list and each sentence immediately. For example, you may write "4 of 7" and underline the correctly spelled words immediately after writing a dictated sentence.

[1] https://youtu.be/pYuOPWRKn-Y is a video of a complete lesson demonstrating how to present blending, segmenting, and each lesson step. At 1 minute 14 seconds you will hear me segmenting sounds for the student to blend. At 9 minutes students begin student worksheet activity [done differently with no worksheet for video purposes]. Reading starts at 12 minutes 50 seconds. Spelling begins at 16 minutes.

Periodically, it is helpful to tell the students a story and ask them to the rewrite it in their own words. I find they love to hear stories about animals, their teacher's childhood, or plans for upcoming events in the school. This eliminates the need for them to generate a story yet requires them to generate sentences. As with dictated sentences, provide immediate feedback regarding the number of words correctly spelled. They also enjoy keeping a graph using colored pencils to track their own progress over time. [See Chapter 11 for graphing chart you can copy and use]. While on the topic of color, most children who are resistant to writing, love to write with colored gel pens. Therefore, I always keep a cup filled with an assortment of colors on the table when meeting face to face.

Strategies for Challenges

What if my student does not match sounds with all the letters?

When students need to develop phoneme [sound] to letter associations for short vowel tones, begin with the CVC short vowel section. This section presents short vowel tones in a hierarchy from widest opening of the jaw position moving to a closed jaw position. Refer to Chapter 11 mouth photos for help showing children how to 'see' the sounds. When we show the student how to 'feel' and 'see' sounds at the same time they hear the sounds, it will help them to stabilize tone recognition and link the sound with the letter thus helping them to read and spell words with more accuracy. You may find that the same students who struggle with matching short vowel tones to letters also do not like to sing and cannot sing a melody on key! Singing tones to blend them, as a model and as an exercise, may be a useful strategy at this skill level. Modify familiar tunes like "Twinkle, Twinkle Little Star" or "Row, Row, Row Your Boat."

Another strategy for short vowel tone recognition is the sentence "Is Eddy at Uncle Ollie's." [Chapter 11] the sound at the beginning of each word is a short vowel tone. The tones present from jaw closed with tongue high to jaw open with tongue low. The following story helps children to understand the sound to words and letters connection.

Is Eddy At Uncle Ollie's?

What if my student does not say all the sounds in a word?

At CVC level, I rarely see this problem, but it does often show up when we introduce CCVC and CVCC syllables.   You can get flat marbles, like florists use in flower arrangements, for this problem. I will take 5 or 6 marbles and slide them for the sounds, taking sounds in and out of the words and switching the positions of the sounds. Chapter 11 contains tables of words that can be used for deleting and inserting sounds to create new words. I have used this for demonstrating and modeling, teaching, and testing for progress for many years. This works best when paired with writing a few of the words at the end of your session. Be aware that you will be departing from the usual lesson structure on the day that this strategy is used. However, it will be much easier to go back to the typical lesson format when the student has a better understanding of the movement of sounds in, out and within words. Keep in mind that it will only take one or two sessions with this activity to see tremendous improvement. Video demonstration: https://youtu.be/r7uoSHkdWAE

What if handwriting is challenging and my student takes too long or refuses to write?

Pick your battles! Remember the goal is to improve reading and spelling and not to teach handwriting. I have found two ways to approach this:

Use graph paper with ½ inch squares for each SOUND. That means some sounds will use 2 or 3 letters within one square on the paper. AND/OR

Either purchase or make letter tiles or cards. Scrabble letters work well or sets of letter tiles can be purchased from educational supply stores or Amazon. I often just use index cards with a list of the letters from our list for that day written on them, but I also like to have enough copies of each letter so that they can 'write' all of the words without taking letters away from the words they have already 'written.' It is important for them to see their success at the end. Keep it simple, you will not need to have the entire alphabet out for any list.   Children rarely object to using the tiles or cards to complete the spelling task.

Graph paper for writing sounds within boxes can be found in Chapter 11.

Letters for printing, cutting, and using to assemble words instead of writing are in Chapter 11

What if my student confuses lower case 'b' and 'd'?

Many teachers and parents believe that the reversal of 'b' and 'd' when writing is a symptom of dyslexia.[1] I would disagree. I find that it is more a symptom of the overall confusion some children encounter when attempting to develop phonemic mapping and processing skills. Trying to make sense of which sounds go with which letters AND how many sounds are in a word AND remembering how and when to write capital and lower case letters AND how to punctuate AND phonic rules for spelling different sound combinations... AND....you get the idea. Somehow mixing up 'b' and' 'd' seems rather normal!

To help your student, emphasize that the sound /b/ begins with the lips together, the letter is written with the line first [represents lips together], and the 'air bump' comes after the line in a left to right progression. Model writing the letter while you explain and speak the sound. Likewise, tell them if they do not feel their lips come together when speaking the /d/ sound, then the 'air bump' comes first and the line second in a left to right progression. They will soon stop reversing /b/ and /d/ when writing. For this strategy to work, it is imperative that they speak the sounds in the words as they are writing them, at least sub-vocally with mouth movement. See Chapter 11.

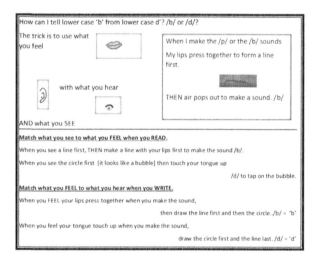

How can I tell lower case 'b' from lower case d'? /b/ or /d/?

The trick is to use what you feel

with what you hear

AND what you SEE

When I make the /p/ or the /b/ sounds

My lips press together to form a line first.

THEN air pops out to make a sound. /b/

Match what you see to what you FEEL when you READ.

When you see a line first, THEN make a line with your lips first to make the sound /b/.

When you see the circle first [it looks like a bubble] then touch your tongue up

/d/ to tap on the bubble.

Match what you FEEL to what you hear when you WRITE.

When you FEEL your lips press together when you make the sound,

then draw the line first and then the circle../b/ = 'b'

When you feel your tongue touch up when you make the sound,

draw the circle first and the line last. /d/ = 'd'

[1]Dyslexia is a term used by many people for disorders that involve difficulty in learning to read or understand words, letters, and numbers when there is no evidence of intellectual disability or other reason for struggling to read and write present.

What if my student wants to know when to use the letters 'c' and 'k' when spelling?

For many children the letter 'c' is confusing. It is 'interchangeable' with the letters 'k' and 's.' Therefore, how can they know which letter to choose when writing words containing the 'k' sound?

Here are some guidelines that will help, although they are not absolute every time. However, the guidelines are reliable for most words having the 'k' sound.

Rules for the letters 'c' and 'k'

1. Usually, words having the initial /s/ just before the letters 'I' 'e' or 'y' will often begin with the letter 'c' instead of the letter 's'---but not always.
2. Where the first sound is /s/ and the next letter is 'a' 'o' 'u' or another consonant, the first letter will be 's'.
3. When the sound /k/ begins a word and the second letter is 'I' 'e' or 'y', then the /k/ sound will be the letter 'k'. Why? Because the letters 'I' 'e' and 'y' turn the letter 'c' into the /s/ sound.
4. When the first sound is /k/ and the second letter is 'a' 'o' 'u' or another consonant, then the first letter will often be 'c'. See the chart of words in Chapter 11 for more help with this.

What about Two Letter Vowels and Consonants?

[Vowel Digraphs] two letters for one vowel sound --i.e., ea, ee, ai, oa, and Diphthongs [two letters representing a vowel sound that is neither long nor short – i.e.: ou, ow, oy, oi, aw] See a list of words in Chapter 11 in the Vowel Combinations Chart.

Vowels with two letters sometimes follow a predictable pattern for when they occur in words or where they might occur. For example, when 'ch' is on the end of a word and there is a long vowel in the word, 'oa' is used for the long vowel sound of 'o' and /ee/ or /ea/ are used for the long vowel sound for /e/. Teach, Coach, Reach, Poach, etc. [See Chapter 11]

When the 'ow' sound as in 'down' is written, it can be in either the middle or end of a word, but the 'ou' sound as in 'round' is always in the middle as in 'found', 'sound' and usually paired with the letter 'n'. See Chapter 11 for lists of alternative vowel spellings.

What if my student does not know when to write '-ed 'or '-d' on the end of a past tense word?

Refer to Chapter 11 for lesson to help with adding the past tense -ed.

Video: https://youtu.be/r7uoSHkdWAE

What if my child reverses 'r' and 'l' letters and sounds in blends?

This is a common area of difficulty for struggling readers and spellers. Chapter 8 includes a section of lists for this problem. Also refer to the video using marbles and letters.

Video: https://youtu.be/r7uoSHkdWAE

CHAPTER 6

CVC Short Vowel | 1-10
Labials, Alveolar, Voiced and Voiceless Pairs
p, b, t, d, m, n, s, l, w

List One: p, b, d, d, m with short a and o:
tab, tap, dap, map, mop, mod, mad, bad, bod, bot

List Two: p, b, t, d, m, w with short a and i and includes irregular spelling with 'tt':
bam, bad, bid, did, dip, whip, whap, map, mat, mitt

List Three: p, b, t, d, m, n with short e and i:
pip, pep, pet, bet, bed, bid, bin, Ben, bet, met

List Four: p, b, t, d, m with short a and u:
tum, tub, dub, pub, pup, Pap, pat, putt, but, bat

List Five: p, b, t, d, m with short a and e:
map, mat, met, med, mad, bad, bed, bet, pet pat

List Six: p, b, t, d, m, n with short u and i:
mud, dud, bud, bid, bit, but, mutt, mitt, pit, pin

List Seven: b, t, d, n, m, s with short u and e -- *FLOSS rule [see phonic chart]*:
set, met, Mel, mull, dull, dell, bell, bet, but, nut

List Eight: p, b, d, m, n with short e and o:
pep, pen, pawn, pod, nod, Ned, med, mod, mop, bop

List Nine: b, t, m, n with short o and u and introduces the concept of silent 'b':
top, tot, Tom, tum, numb, bum, bomb, bot, not, nut

List Ten: b, t, d, l, m with short o and i and includes the concept of silent 'b':
dip, tip, top, bop, lop, lip, limb, Tim, Tom, mom

CVC Labials, Alveolar, Voiced and Voiceless Pairs
Lists One to Ten Reading Page -- p, b, t, d, m, n, s, l, w

List One:

tab, tap, dap, map, mop, mod, mad, bad, bod, bot

List Two:

bam, bad, bid, did, dip, whip, whap, map, mat, mitt

List Three:

pip, pep, pet, bet, bed, bid, bin, Ben, bet, met

List Four:

tum, tub, dub, pub, pup, Pap, pat, putt, but, bat

List Five:

map, mat, met, med mad, bad, bed, bet, pet pat

List Six:

mud, dud, bud, bid, bit, but, mutt, mitt, pit, pin

List Seven:

set, met, Mel, mull, dull, dell, bell, bet, but, nut

List Eight:

pep, pen, pawn, pod, nod, Ned, med, mod, mop, bop

List Nine:

top, tot, Tom, tum, numb, bum, bomb, bot, not, nut

List Ten:

dip, tip, top, bop, lop, lip, limb, Tim, Tom, mom

CVC Labials, Alveolar, Voiced and Voiceless Pairs
p, b, t, d, m, n, s, l, w
Sentences for Reading and Dictation for Lists One to Ten

1. Tom had a pit and bit his lip.

2. Ross was boss of the bus and the jet.

3. Dip the tip of the limb in the well.

4. Mom put a dull pin in the map.

5. Ned bet a bat set on Ben to win.

6. Tom put a nut, a bat, and a pen on the mat.

7. Dad has a pen, and a pawn, but not a nut.

8. Mel put the nut in the mud.

9. Tim met Ned by the net with Bud.

10. Set the mitt and the tab on top of the bed

 .

CVC Short Vowel | 11-20
Labials, Alveolar, Palatals, Dentals
Voiced and Voiceless Pairs
p, b, m, n, f, v, l, r, t, d, ch, sh, s, th, j, g, w

List Eleven: b, j, r, with short a and o *–tch phonic rule for short vowels:*
botch, batch, bam, jam, jab, job, lob, rob, Bob, Bab

List Twelve: p, b, t, m, w, s, sh, th with short a and i -- *the FLOSS rule:*
wish, wit, with, pith, path, bath, bass, mass, miss, myth

List Thirteen: b, t, d, w, f, n, l and t, m, l, s, sh, ch, j with short e and i *FLOSS, -tch:*
nib, fib, fit, wit, lit, let, wet, wed, fed, Feb
mess, mesh, met, mitt, Mitch, miss, mill, Jill, gel, jet

List Fourteen: p, b, m, n, f, l, ch, j with short a and u *–dge rule, -tch and FLOSS:*
fuzz, fudge, judge, nudge, budge, badge, batch, patch, latch, match

List Fifteen: p, m, n, w, v, s, ch, j with short a and e -- *FLOSS rule and the   second sound of 'g' [see phonic rule chart]:*
Pam, jam, gem, Jess, chess, Wes, when, men, man, van

List Sixteen: m, l, f, s, z, th, ch with short u and i – includes the FLOSS rule:
sis, this, thus, muss, fuss, fuzz, fizz, fill, chill, mill

List Seventeen: b, t, d, v, n, r, with short u and e: - includes –dge and silent   w
nut, net, vet, bet, but, budge, bud, bed, red, wren

List Eighteen: m, l, f, s, ch, j with short e and o—*includes the FLOSS rule:*
fess, less, loss, moss, mess, chess, Chet, jet, jot, lot

List Nineteen: b, t, n, r, s with short o and u- *includes FLOSS rule*
not, rot, rut, rub, rob, Ross, boss, bus, but, bot

 List Twenty: b, t, m, f, l, s, z, sh, r with short o and i- *includes FLOSS rule:*
miss, moss, Ross, boss, loss, lot, lit, fit, fizz, fish

*Two lists are included due to frequent intense need for discrimination between short /e/ and/ i/ phonemes

CVC Labials, Alveolar, Palatals, Dentals
Voiced and Voiceless Pairs
p, b, m, n, f, v, l, r, t, d, ch, sh, s, th, j, g, w
Lists Eleven to Twenty Reading Page

List Eleven:

botch, batch, bam, jam, jab, job, lob, rob, Bob, Bab

List Twelve:

wish, wit, with, pith, path, bath, bass, mass, miss, myth

List Thirteen:

nib, fib, fit, wit, lit, let, wet, wed, fed, Feb
mess, mesh, met, mitt, Mitch, miss, mill, Jill, gel, jet

List Fourteen:

fuzz, fudge, judge, nudge, budge, badge, batch, patch, latch, match

List Fifteen:

Pam, jam, gem, Jess, chess, Wes, when, men, man, van

List Sixteen:

sis, this, thus, muss, fuss, fuzz, fizz, fill, chill, mill

List Seventeen:

nut, net, vet, bet, but, budge, bud, bed, red, wren

List Eighteen:

fess, less, loss, moss, mess, chess, Chet, jet, jot, lot

List Nineteen:

not, rot, rut, rub, rob, Ross, boss, bus, but, bot

List Twenty:

miss, moss, Ross, boss, loss, lot, lit, fit, fizz, fish

CVC Labials, Alveolar, Palatals, Dentals
Voiced and Voiceless Pairs
p, b, m, n, f, l, r, t, d, ch, sh, s, th, j, g, w
Sentences for Reading and Dictation
Lists Eleven to Twenty

1. Jess let Chet check the chess set.

2. Ross was boss of the bus and the jet.

3. This fish will not budge to miss the moss.

4. The mess is less on the lot.

5. Patch the latch then match the fudge.

6. Fill and chill the cup with fizz and fuzz.

7. Mitch will miss Jill at the mill.

8. Bob will jam the batch of fudge in the jet.

9. I wish Bab did not fuss with Chet.

10. The vet bet his check on the pet.

CVC Short Vowel | 21-30
Velars, Alveolar, Palatals
k, g, t, d, n, l, sh, ch, j, r

List Twenty-One: t, d, g, k [c] with short a and o:
cot, cod, cad, tad, tag, tog, Todd, God, got, dot

List Twenty-Two: t, r, k [c], g, sh with short a and i *–ck phonic rule and silent w*:
gal, gad, rad, rack, Rick, rid, writ, rat, cat, cash

List Twenty-Three: t, d, l, r, k, g, j with short e and i: *–ck, FLOSS, two sounds g*:
deck, dell, tell, gel, Jill, jig, rig, rid, lid, lick

List Twenty-four: g, l, r, sh with short a and u:
lug, lag, gag, shag, rag, rug, rut, gut, gull, lull

List Twenty-Five: t, d, k, g, l, sh with short a and e *-ck rule:*
shed, shad, lad, led, let, leg, lag, shag, shack, knack

List Twenty-Six: t, l, r, k [c], g with short u and i- *–ck rule*:
cud, kid, rid, rig, rug, lug, luck, tuck, chuck, chick

List Twenty-Seven: d, l, k, g, sh, ch with short u and e: *-ck and FLOSS:*
check, deck, duck, dull, gull, gush, rush, lush, lug, leg

List Twenty- Eight: t, d, l, k, g, ch with short e and o: *-ck and FLOSS*:
cog, keg, leg, log, dog, doll, tall, talk, chock, check

List Twenty-Nine: t, d, n, k [c], g, sh, j with short o and u:
nut, not, cot, shot, jot, jut, shut, gut, cut, cud

List Thirty: t, d, l, k, r with short o and i: *–ck rule*:
kick, kit, lit, lid, rid, rod, rock, Rick, lick, lock

CVC   Velars, Alveolar, Palatals
k, g, t, d, n, l, sh, ch, j, r
Lists Twenty-One to Thirty Reading Page

List Twenty-One:

cot, cod, cad, tad, tag, tog, Todd, God, got, dot

List Twenty-Two:

gal, gad, rad, rack, Rick, rid, writ, rat, cat, cash

List Twenty-Three:

deck, dell, tell, gel, Jill, jig, rig, rid, lid, lick

List Twenty-Four:

lug, lag, gag, shag, rag, rug, rut, gut, gull, lull

List Twenty-Five:

shed, shad, lad, led, let, leg, lag, shag, shack, knack

List Twenty-Six:

cud, kid, rid, rig, rug, lug, luck, tuck, chuck, chick, tick

List Twenty-Seven:

check, deck, duck, dull, gull, gush, rush, lush, lug, leg

List Twenty-Eight:

cog, keg, leg, log, dog, doll, tall, talk, chock, check

List Twenty-Nine:

nut, not, cot, shot, jot, jut, shut, gut, cut, cud

List Thirty:

kick, kit, lit, lid, rid, rod, rock, Rick, lick, lock

CVC   Velars, Alveolar, Palatals
k, g, t, d, n, l, sh, ch, j, r,

Sentences for Reading and Dictation for Lists Twenty-One to Thirty

1. Rick can rock into the lid to get rid of the rat.

2. A kid cannot gut a cod fish.

3. The dog had a keg with a cog on its neck.

4. The duck and the gull can rush to check the shed.

5. Chuck had a chick with a tick on it.

6. Put the shad in the shed and the cod in the shack.

7. Todd can lug a rat and a gull to the deck.

8. Jill put a lid and a deck on the rig.

9. The gal with Rick got rid of his cat and his cash.

10. The cot for the cod was a tad too much.

CVC Short Vowel | 31-40
Dentals, Alveolar, Palatals
Voiced and Voiceless Pairs
sh, th, ch, j, s, z, f

Note: No distinction is made between voiced and voiceless /th/ for auditory tracking. The sounds are both spelled the same, so for tracking purposes we do not distinguish. However, discussion may arise so discuss how they are spelled the same, but sound different because the voice is turned on or off.

List Thirty-One: sh, s, ch short vowels /i/ /a/ /o/: *–ck rule*
ship, chip, chap, sap, sop, chop, shop, shock, sock, sick

List Thirty-Two: sh, s, ch short vowels /u/ /i/ /a/: - tch FLOSS rule
such, Dutch, ditch, pitch, patch, batch, bash, dash, dish, dill

List Thirty-Three: th, f, j short vowels /i/ /a//o/ /u/:
thin, then, than, fan, fat, bat, bath, badge, budge, fudge

List Thirty-Four: sh, s, j, th, short vowels /i/ /e/ /a/: FLOSS rule
Jill, gel, sell, shell, shall, Sal, sad, said, shed, Jed

List Thirty-Five: sh, s, z, ch, th short vowels /i/ /u/: *–ck rule*
zip, sip, sis, this, thick, chick, chuck, shuck, shush, mush

List Thirty-Six: sh, f, j, ch short vowel /u/ /a/ /o/ s: tch *rule* -dge rule –
much, muff, Mudge, Madge, match, thatch, hatch, latch, lash, laugh

List Thirty-Seven: sh, s, th f short vowels/u/ /a/ /e/: -dge rule – FLOSS rule
judge, fudge, Mudge, Madge, badge, bash, bath, Beth, Seth, sell

List Thirty-Eight: sh, f, j ch short vowels /e/ /i/ /o/: – FLOSS rule
shall, shell, fell, fill, fin, chin, gin, Jon, jot, jet

List Thirty-Nine: th, s, short vowels /e/ /a/ /u/: – FLOSS rule
Chet, chess, mess, mesh, mash, mass, pass, path, pith, with,

List Forty: sh, ch, th short vowels /o/ /a/ /i/: –tch *rule*
wish, which, watch, botch, notch, natch, match, math, myth, pith

CVC   Dentals, Alveolar, Palatals
Voiced and Voiceless Pairs
sh, th, ch, j, s, z, f
Lists Thirty-One to Forty Reading Page

List Thirty-One

ship, chip, chap, sap, sop, chop, shop, shock, sock, sick

List Thirty-Two

such, Dutch, ditch, pitch, patch, batch, bash, dash, dish, dill

List Thirty-Three:

thin, fan, then, that, bat, bath, path, pass, patch, latch

List Thirty-Four

Jill, gel, sell, shell, Seth, said, shed, Jed, Zed, fed

List Thirty-Five

zip, sip, sis, this, thick, chick, chuck, shuck, shush, mush

List Thirty-Six

much, muff, Mudge, Madge, match, thatch, hatch, latch, lash, laugh

List Thirty-Seven

judge, fudge, Mudge, Madge, badge, bash, bath, Beth, Seth, sell

List Thirty-Eight

shell, fell, fill, fin, chin, gin, Jon, jot, jet set

List Thirty-Nine:

Chet, chess, mess, mesh, mash, mass, pass, path, pith, with

Chet, chess, mess, mesh, mash, mash, mass, pass, path, pith

List Forty:

wish, which, watch, botch, notch, natch, match, math, myth, pith

CVC Dentals, Alveolar, Palatals
Voiced and Voiceless Pairs
sh, th, ch, j, s, z, f

Sentences for Reading and Dictation for
Lists Thirty-One to Forty

1. He went to shop for a sock on the ship.

2. Jill made a Dutch dish for the bash.

3. It was a job to give the fat bat a bath on the thin path.

4. Zed said Jill put gel in the shell.

5. Sis will try to zip mush in bag with the chick.

6. Madge put too much thatch by the thatch to the gate.

7. Beth wants to sell fudge to the judge.

8. Jot this down, "Jon fell on a shell."

9. Will you pass Chet playing chess on the path?

10. I wish I could watch but I must do math.

Long and Short Vowel Word Lists for CVC Words

CVC 1-10 | Long and Short Vowels
Labials, Alveolar,
Voiced and Voiceless Pairs
p, b, m, n, f, l, r, t, d, ch, sh, s, th, j, g, w

List One: p, t, d, m, k with a and o - *introducing short o as [-al-] and final e:*
tape, tap, tack, take, talk, top, mop, mope, map, mad

List Two: p, b, d, n with a and i - *final e and [-ie-]:*
bid, bad, bade, bide, died, did, dip, din, Dane, dine

List Three: p, b, t, d, n, l with e and i - *final e, [-ee-], and [-ea-]:*
pipe, peep, Pete, beet, bet, bed, Ben, bean, lean, line

List Four: p, b, t, d, l, with a and u -- *final e and [-oo-]:*
tub, tube, lube, loop, dupe, poop, pup, Pap, pat, pate

List Five: b, t, d, m, with a and e --*final e, [-ee-]*
mate, meet, met, med, mad, made, bade, bad, bed, bet

List Six: b, t, d u and i - *final e, [-ie-], [oo]:*
dud, dude, died, did, bid, bide, bite, boot, but, bud

List Seven: t, d, m, l, s with u and e - *FLOSS, [-ea-], [ee]:*
seat, set, met, meet, mutt, mull, mule, Mel, meal, deal

List Eight: p, t, d, f, l with e and o - *final e, [-au-], [-ee-], [-ea-], -al-]:*
peep, peal, pole, Paul, tall, teal, tell, fell, fed, feed

List Nine: b, t, m, n with short o and u - *[-oo-] and final e:*
tote, toot, tot, Tom, tome, tone, tune, boon, bun, bum

List Ten: w, l, m, n with o and i - *final e, silent b and [y] for short i:*
Nome, dome, Dom, dim, dime, lime, limb, Lynn, line, wine

CVC Long and Short Vowels with Labials, Alveolar,
Voiced and Voiceless Pairs
p, b, m, n, f, l, r, t, d, ch, sh, s, th, j, g, w
Lists One through Ten Reading Page

List One:

tape, tap, tack, take, talk, top, mop, mope, map, mad

List Two:

bid, bad, bade, bide, died, did, dip, din, Dane, dine

List Three:

pipe, peep, Pete, beet, bet, bed, Ben, bean, lean, line

List Four:

tub, tube, lube, loop, dupe, poop, pup, Pap, pat, pate

List Five:

mate, meet, met, med, mad, made, bade, bad, bed, bet

List Six:

dud, dude, died, did, bid, bide, bite, boot, but, bud

List Seven.

seat, set, met, meet, mutt, mull, mule, Mel, meal, deal

List Eight:

peep, peal, pole, Paul, tall, teal, tell, fell, fed, feed

List Nine:

tote, toot, tot, Tom, tome, tone, tune, boon, bun, bum

List Ten:

Nome, dome, Dom, dim, dime, lime, limb, Lynn, line, wine

**CVC Long and Short Vowels with Labials, Alveolar,
Voiced and Voiceless Pairs
p, b, t, d, m, n, s, l, w
Sentences for Reading and Dictation Lists One through Ten**

1. Dan put tape on the mop that he made.

2. Dane will bide his time to dine with you.

3. Pete and Ben put a pipeline in the mine.

4. Pap put a loop of tube in the tub.

5. The shipmate Mel met made him mad.

6. The dude did bite his boot!

7. Mel sat in his seat to eat a meal with the mule.

8. Tell Paul that the tall pole fell.

9. At the toot of the tone the bun will be done.

10. Dom said, "Nope, I will not dip the dime in the lime."

CVC 11-20 | Long and Short Vowels
Labials, Alveolar, Palatals, Dentals
With Long and Short Vowels
p, b, m, w, n, f, [ph], v, l, r, t, d, ch, sh, s, th, j, g,

List Eleven: b, t, d, l, m, n, r, sh, j with a and o: - *final e rule:*
dame, lame, shame, tame, tam, Tom, tome, tone, moan, main

List Twelve: m, t, d, r with a and i: - *[-igh-], [-ai-], and [-ce-]:*
rid, **rad**, **raid**, **race**, **rate**, **right**, **might**, **mate**, **made, mare**

List Thirteen: t, m, l, s, ch, with e and i: *[-ce-], [-igh-], [-ea-], [-ee], and FLOSS:*
met, **meet**, **might**, **mitt**, **Mitch**, **miss**, **mice**, **mess**, **less**, **lease**

List Fourteen: t, m, z, f, v, j, with a and u – *[-oo-], [-ph-] and vowel effect on s and z:*
fuzz, fuse, phase, raise, rage, rave, rate, root, room, zoom

List Fifteen: p, m, n, v, r, j and t, n, l, sh, j *with a and e: two lists for extra practice*
–final e, [-ea,], [-ai,]; and final e [-ee-], -ea-], [-ai-], FLOSS*
them, gem, jam, Jan, van, vane, pane, rain, mane, mean,

sheen, teen, ten, Jen, jean, Jane, jail, shale, shall, shell

List Sixteen: l, m, f, s, z. sh, ch with u and i- *final e, [-oo-], FLOSS, and vowel effect on s and z:*
muse, shoes, choose, fuse, fizz, fill, file mile, mice, miss

List Seventeen: b, t, d, sh, ch, j with u and e: *[-oo-], [-ee-], -dge, [-ea-], -ch with long vowel:*
shoot, shut, sheet, beet, bet, but, budge, bud, bead, beach

List Eighteen: t, d, l, n, s, r with e and o: - *[-ee-], [-ea-], [-oa-], FLOSS, and vowel effect on s and z:*
leech, lead, led, load, toad, Todd, toss, Ross, rose, nose

List Nineteen: t, d, n, r with short o and u: - *silent w, final e [-oo-]:*
nut, not, note, wrote, rot, rut, root, rude, rode, rod

List Twenty: p, m, f, s, r with o and i: *[-igh-], [-ce], FLOSS, and vowel effect on s and z:*
fight, sight, sit, sis, miss, mice, rice, Ross, rose, pose
 *Two lists because students often need more help with hearing differences for short e and i

CVC Labials, Alveolar, Palatals, Dentals
With Long and Short Vowels
p, b, m, w, n, f, [ph], v, l, r, t, d, ch, sh, s, th, j, g,
Lists Eleven through Twenty Reading Page

List Eleven:

dame, lame, shame, tame, tam, Tom, tome, tone, moan, main

List Twelve:

rid, rad, raid, race, rate, right, might, mate, mat

List Thirteen:

met, meet, might, mitt, Mitch, miss, mice, mess, less, lease

List Fourteen:

fuzz, fuse, phase, raise, rage, rave, rate, root, room, zoom

List Fifteen:
them, gem, jam, Jan, van, vane, pane, rain, mane, mean
sheen, teen, ten, Jen, jean, Jane, jail, shale, shall, shell

List Sixteen:

muse, shoes, choose, fuse, fizz, fill, file mile, mice, miss

List Seventeen:

shoot, shut, sheet, beet, bet, but, budge, bud, bead, beach

List Eighteen:

leech, lead, led, load, toad, Todd, toss, Ross, rose, nose

List Nineteen:

nut, not, note, wrote, rot, rut, root, rude, rode, rod

List Twenty:

fight, sight, sit, sis, miss, mice, rice, Ross, rose, pose

CVC   Labials, Alveolar, Palatals, Dentals
With Long and Short Vowels
p, b, m, w, n, f, [ph], v, l, r, t, d, ch, sh, s, th, j, g
Sentences for Reading and Dictation Lists Eleven through Twenty

1. Jan and Tom did put the tame roan horse in the race.

2. At this rate, the mate might win the race.

3. Mitch might meet the mice that made the mess.

4. The root had room to raise the roof.

5. Jen and Jane drove the van in the rain.

6. If you choose those shoes, you might fuss with the fuzz on them.

7. The jail is shut and will not budge.

8. I choose the rose with a toad on it.

9. Ross rode a toad in the race with the leech.

10. Mitch and the mice will fight for the rice.

CVC 21-30 | Long and Short Vowels
Velars, Alveolar, Palatals, Dentals
With Long and Short Vowels
k, g, t, d, n, l, sh, ch, j, r, th, f, v

List Twenty-One: t, d, f, k [c], l, r with a and o: -*[-ough-], [-oa-], [-al-], [-ol-], final e:*
cot, **coat**, **code**, **cod**, **cough**, **call**, **kale**, **coal**, **roll**, **rode**

List Twenty-Two: t, d, k [c], g, r, l with a and i: - *[-ai-], [-igh-], -ck, final e:*
gale, rail, rake, rack, Rick, rid, ride, right, kite, Kate

List Twenty-Three: d, n, l, s, ch, r with and i and e: - *[-ee-], [-ea-], silent w, -ck:*
deck, wreck, reek, seek, cheek, leak, lick, chick, check, neck

List Twenty-Four: m, t, l, s, sh, h, k [c], g, with a and u: *[-oo-], [-ui-], final e:*
hut, hat, hoot, shoot, suit, lute, late, Kate, cute, mute

List Twenty-Five: d, k, s, sh, ch with a and e: *[-ee-], [-ea-], -ck, final e, and long vowel with –ch:*
shack, shake, sake, sack, seek, seed, said, red, reed, reach

List Twenty-Six: t, d, k, g, with u and i: *-ck, and final e:*
tuck, tick, tike, like, lick, luck, Luke, Duke, duck, dug

List Twenty-Seven: t, d, l, f, j, r with u and e*: [-ue-], [-ea-], [-oo-], FLOSS, [-ew-] and final e:*
fell, fuel, jewel, duel, dell, dead, fed, red, rude, root

List Twenty-Eight: t, d, k, ch, r with e and o*: [-ee-], [-oa-], final e, -ck, silent w:*
Cheek, choke, check, deck, wreck, red, reed, rode, toad, code

List Twenty-Nine: t, n, k [c], sh, th, r, j with short o and u- *[-oa-], [-ough-], [-oo-], and final e:*
note, coat, cot, thought, shot, shoot, root, rot, jot, jute

List Thirty: p, t, d, l, k, r with o and i: - *[-igh-] and final e:*
kit, kite, light, lit, lid, rid, ride, rode, rope, ripe

Velars, Alveolar, Palatals, Dentals
With Long and Short Vowels
k, g, t, d, n, l, sh, ch, j, r, th, f, v
Lists Twenty-One to Thirty Reading Page

List Twenty-One:
cot, coat, code, cod, cough, call, kale, coal, roll, rode

List Twenty-Two:
gale, rail, rake, rack, Rick, rid, ride, right, kite, Kate

List Twenty-Three:
deck, wreck, reek, seek, cheek, leak, lick, chick, check, neck

List Twenty-Four:
hut, hat, hoot, shoot, suit, lute, late, Kate, cute, mute

List Twenty-Five
shack, shake, sake, sack, seek, seed, said, red, reed, reach

List Twenty-Six:
tuck, tick, tike, like, lick, luck, Luke, Duke, duck, dug,

List Twenty-Seven:
fell, fuel, jewel, duel, dell, dead, fed, red, rude, root

List Twenty: Eight:
Cheek, choke, check, deck, wreck, red, reed, rode, toad

List Twenty-Nine:
note, coat, cot, thought, shot, shoot, root, rot, jot, jute

List Thirty:
kit, kite, light, lit, lid, rid, ride, rode, rope, ripe

Velars, Alveolar, Palatals, Dentals
k, g, t, d, n, l, sh, ch, j, r, th, f, v
With Long and Short Vowels
Sentences for Reading and Dictation Lists Twenty-One through Thirty

1. He put the coat and the kale on the cot.

2. Rick got rid of the kite and the cat.

3. Check the chick on the deck with the leak.

4. Mute the TV in the hut for cute Kate the cat.

5. Reach in the shack and shake the sack.

6. Luke and Duck like to lick duck.

7. A dude in the dell was in a duel for a jewel.

8. The toad did choke on the reed by the hot deck.

9. Jot a note on the jute shoot.

10. Ride the kite that you made with the kit.

CVC 31-40 | Long and Short Vowels
CVC   Dentals, Alveolar, Palatals
Voiced and Voiceless Pairs
sh, th, ch, j, s, z, f

List Thirty-One: sh, ch   with long ee and a: *featuring 'ea' and, ee'*
Shape, shade, she'd, chic [*pronounced sheek*] cheek, cheat, sheet, Pete, peach, teach

List Thirty-Two: j, sh, s with long e, a, o u: *featuring 'ee' and 'oa'*
Jeep, sheep, shape, shake, sake, Jake, juke, joke, soak, seek

List Thirty-Three: th, s, f, sh, j with long e and a *featuring 'i.e.,' 'ea' 'ee' 'ai 'and contraction*
Thieve, sieve, seat, feet, feed, she'd, sheath, she'll, shale, jail

List Thirty-Four: s, j, ch, sh with long a and I *featuring -ce and 'ai'*
Sage wage, page, rage, race, rain, chain, Shane, shine, shone

List Thirty-Five: th, s, f, sh, j with long e i o and o: *featuring 'ee' Ie' 'ea' and 'oa'*
Theme, seem, sieve, thieve, thief, sheaf, sheen, shine, shone, Joan

List Thirty-Six: j, ch with long and short a and o: *featuring -dge -tch 'oa'*
Page, cage, sage, wage, rage, ridge, rich, pitch, poach, roach

List Thirty-Seven: f, s, j, th with long e i u and short i: *featuring 'ee' -igh- -oo- -ui- -ce*
Feet, fight, light, lute, loose, juice, moose, mice, miss, myth

List Thirty-Eight: ch, sh, j, z and f with long e and short e I u: *featuring 'ea'–tch Floss -dge*
Peach, reach, wretch, fetch, Feb, fib, fish, fizz, fuzz, fudge

List Thirty-Nine: z, sh, ch with short o long e and o: *featuring -ause, -aws, -ows, 'ee' 'ea'*
Pause, cause, thaws, laws, lows, nose, shows, she's, sheet, cheat

List Forty: j and s with long u a and e: *featuring 'ai' 'ea' and -ce*
jute, Jude, juke, Jake, jail, wail, wage, page, pace, peace

CVC   Dentals, Alveolar, Palatals
Voiced and Voiceless Pairs
sh, th, ch, j, s, z, f
Lists Thirty-One to Forty Reading Page

List Thirty-One:
Shape, shade, she'd, chic *[pronounced sheek]* cheek, cheat, sheet, Pete, peach, teach

List Thirty-Two:
Jeep, sheep, shape, shake, sake, Jake, juke, joke, soak, seek

List Thirty-Three:
Thieve, sieve, seat, feet, feed, she'd, sheath, she'll, shale, jail

List Thirty-Four:
Sage wage, page, rage, race, rain, chain, Shane, shine, shone

List Thirty-Five:
Theme, seem, sieve, thieve, thief, sheaf, sheen, shine, shone, Joan

List Thirty-Six:
Page, cage, sage, wage, rage, ridge, rich, pitch, poach, roach

List Thirty-Seven:
Feet, fight, light, lute, loose, juice, moose, mice, miss, myth

List Thirty-Eight:
Peach, reach, wretch, fetch, Feb, fib, fish, fizz, fuzz, fudge

List Thirty-Nine:
Pause, cause, thaws, laws, lows, nose, shows, she's, sheet, cheat

List Forty:
jute, Jude, juke, Jake, jail, wail, wage, page, pace, peace

CVC   Dentals, Alveolar, Palatals
Voiced and Voiceless Pairs
sh, th, ch, j, s, z, f
Sentences for Reading and Dictation Lists Thirty-one to Forty

1. Pete got a peach in the shade of the tree.

2. He took the sheep for a shave in the jeep for a joke.

3. Shane made a wage from the sale of the shale.

4. The sheen on the jeep shone in even in the shade.

5. The roach in the cage was the theme of the day.

6. It is a myth that moose and mice like juice.

7. There is fuzz on the fudge but not on the fish.

8. I choose the rose with a toad on it.

9. Let's take pause while she shows us the laws.

10. Jake grows jute for a wage and to keep peace.

CHAPTER 7

CCV, CCVC and CVCC SYLLABLES

LONG AND SHORT VOWEL TONES

Reversals

The following list of two phoneme words is used to drill students in the order of motor and phoneme [sound]. Place two marbles of different colors or two small pieces of paper of different shapes before the student. Model the two sounds in different sequences to demonstrate how the order of sounds changes the word.

Please note: the following list is **NOT** a 'one sound change' chain of words. Therefore, the words are not intended for use with the student worksheets. However, the teacher record sheet includes space for recording student number of correct student responses. You may want to use tokens or game turns to count correct responses for reinforcement.

uth = the	zi = is
fo = off	chi = itch
sie = ice	li = ill
oyb =boy	ree = ear
eesh –=she	ni = in
oeg = go	knaw = on
ti = it	own = no
ieb = bye	eek = key
ees = see	koa = oak
eem = me	iet = tie
eat = tea	ire = rye
eeb = be	ied = dye
eep = pea	iep = pie
eef = fee	aed = day
vee = eve	aeth = they
lee = eel	air = ray
een = knee	ace = say
fi = if	ache =kay

/r/ Sound Sequence Instruction

The next three lists cover /r/ reversals. The /r/ sound is a vocalic phoneme that is difficult for many students to sequence. Cues to help include:

Ask the student to think about the position of the vowel tone in relationship to the first consonant.

1. "Does the /r/ sound come right after the first sound {free} or does it come right after the vowel sound {fear}?"
2. "Does the /r/ come right after the first sound {crud} or right before the last sound {curd}?

Tell them to "Think about how your mouth feels when you say the word as well as what you hear. Practice segmenting the sound while touching manipulatives to help the student visualize the location of the /r/ phoneme in the sequence.

Practice Lists for /r/ phoneme reversals

List One CCV and VCC reversals for the /r/ sounds – or:
for, fro, bro, bore, poor, pro, throw, Thor, or, row

Answers for List
When sounds
Reverse Order

List Two One CCV and VCC reversals for the /r/ sounds – air and –ire:
air, rare, fair, fray, tray, tare, tire, try, fry, fire

List Three One CCV and VCC reversals for the /r/ sounds - ear and air:
fear, free, tree, tear, peer, pair, care, cray, crow, core

List Four CCVC and CVCC reversals:
breed, beard, feared, freed, creed, reed, road, crowed, cord, court

On the following page arrows are used with shape changes inserted
Into the shapes to indicate the sound movement. Either method works. Use the method that makes the most sense to the student, and to you.

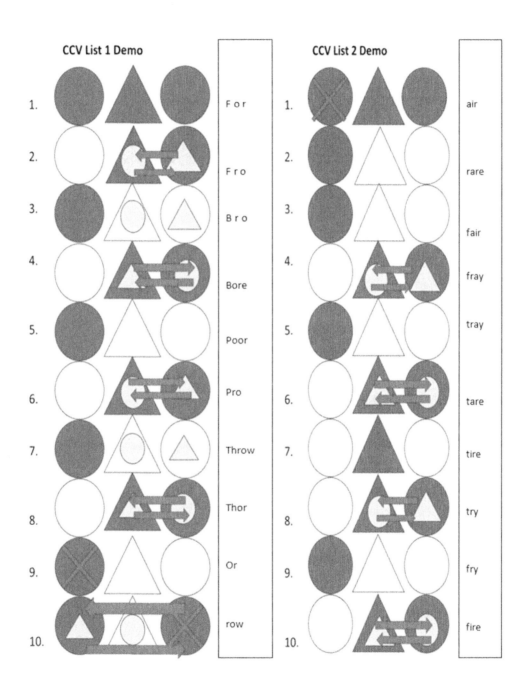

CCV List 1 Demo

1. F o r
2. F r o
3. B r o
4. Bore
5. Poor
6. Pro
7. Throw
8. Thor
9. Or
10. row

CCV List 2 Demo

1. air
2. rare
3. fair
4. fray
5. tray
6. tare
7. tire
8. try
9. fry
10. fire

Practice Lists for /r/ phoneme reversals
Lists One to Four Reading Page

List One CCV and VCC reversals for the /r/ sounds – or:

for, fro, bro, bore, poor, pro, throw, Thor, or, row

List Two One CCV and VCC reversals for the /r/ sounds – air and –ire:

air, rare, fair, fray, tray, tare, tire, try, fry, fire

List Three One CCV and VCC reversals for the /r/ sounds - ear and air:

fear, free, tree, tear, peer, pair, care, cray, crow, core

List Four CCVC and CVCC reversals:

breed, beard, feared, freed, creed, reed, road, crowed, cord, court

Practice Lists for /r/ phoneme reversals

Sentences for Reading and Dictation for /r/ phoneme reversal

Lists One to Four

1. A pro can throw a football to Thor.

2. Is it fair to set a tire on fire and smoke up the air?

3. I fear the three crows will tear up the pair of trees.

4. Poor bro, he cannot throw very far.

5. It is a rare person that can fray their jeans and not tear them.

6. Lend me your ear to hear the story of the free crow in the cray.

7. Plant your corn in a row, bro.

8. It was a fair fight for the friar, but he tore his coat on the tire.

9. Try not to fray the rare cloth.

10. Freedom is never free so we should take care of our freedom.

11. That breed of dog has a beard and should be feared when you see it on the road.

How to Treat Sound Reductions or Deletions

To help students recognize the presence of voiceless sounds and nasals, sometimes words with three sounds rather than four sounds occur when studying CCV, CCVC and CVCC syllables. Within each list, there is only one sound change between each word. Therefore, two shapes may be marked to indicate a missing sound. For example, given the following CCVC exercise example:

> When changing '**bride'** to '**bide,'** the /r/ is missing, so the second circle is marked.
> Then when changing '**bide'** to '**bite,'** the /r/ is still missing, but the last sound also changed, so an **X** is placed in the second circle and the last space is marked.
> When changing '**bite'** to '**bright,'** the /r/ returned, so the second circle is marked.

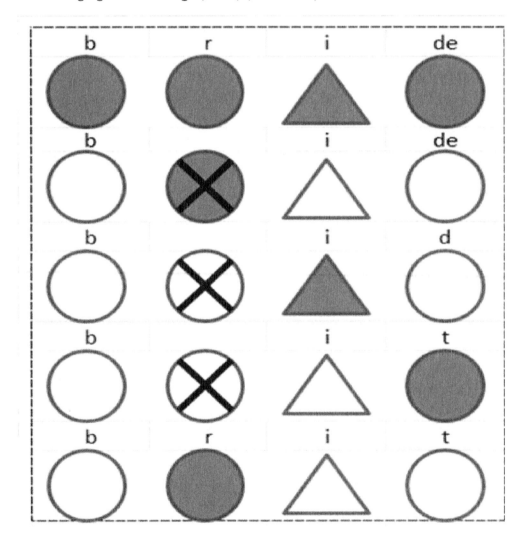

Another example with CVCC:

When changing '**lamp**' to '**lap**' the /m/ is missing, so the second circle is marked.

Then when changing '**lap**' to '**lip**' the /m/ is still missing, so an **X** is placed in the second circle and the second space is marked because the /a/ is now /i/.

When changing '**lip**' to '**limp**', the /m/ is added back so the second circle is marked.

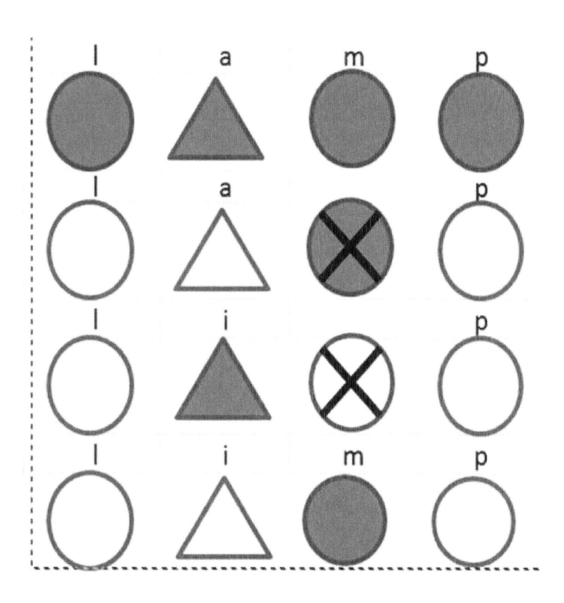

CCV Reversals | 1-10
All Consonant Sounds with Long Vowels
All Consonants and Long Vowels
/s/, /r/ and /l/ Blends

List One: long f, p, k, r, l with long i and a- *long vowel final –y-:*
fly, ply, play, pray, fray, fry, cry, cray, clay, lay

List Two: t, p, l s blends with long i, a, o, and u- *long vowel final –y, -ay, -ow, -ew:*
sty, spy, spay, stay, stew, stow, snow, slow, slew, spew

List Three: b, p, f, l, r with long i, o, u, and a
long vowel final –ew, -ay, -ow; and long vowel –ew, -o, -ow, -y, final e:
brew, bray, ray, fray, fro, flow, foe, few, flew, fly
flew, blue, brew, bro, blow, flow, fro, pro, pry, fry

List Four: b, p, f, t, r, l with long i, a, and e - *-ay, -ow, -ew, -ee, -ea:*
bray, pray, pre, plea, flee, free, tree, tea, pea, plea

List Five: s, f, t, d, l, r with long i, o, and u - *-y, -ow, -ew, final e:*
sly, slow, slew, flew, few, dew, drew, true, try, dry

List Six: th, k, f, r, s with long i, o, u, a, and e- *-ow, -y, -ee, -ough, -ew:*
throw, crow, cry, fry, free, three, through, crew, cue, few

List Seven: d, t, th, f, s with long i, o, u, a, and e- - *-y –ee, -ay, -ow:*
dry, try, tree, three, free, fray, ray, say, slay, slow

List Eight: k, g, r, l with long i, o, u, a, and e- *-ay, - ew, -ay, -ow, -y, final e:*
clay, clue, glue, grew, gray, grow, crow, cry, crew, cue

List Nine: p, b, t, d, r, l with long i, o, u, a, and e- *-ee, -ew, -aw, -y, -ay, final e:*
tree, true, drew, draw, dry, try, tray, bray, pray, play

List Ten: s, l with long i, o, u, a, and e- - *ew, –ee, -ay, –y, –igh- -o, -ow:*
slew, slee, see, say, slay, sly, lie, sigh, so, slow

CCV All Consonant sounds
s, r, l blends
Lists -One to Ten Reading Page

List One:

fly, ply, play, pray, fray, fry, cry, cray, clay, lay

List Two:

sty spy spays stay stew stow snow slow slew spew

List Three:

brew, bray, ray, fray, fro, flow, foe, few, flew, fly
flew, blue, brew, bro, blow, flow, fro, pro, pry, fry

List Four:

bray, pray, pre, plea, flee, free, tree, tea, pea, plea

List Five:

sly, slow, slew, flew, few, dew, drew, true, try, dry

List Six:

throw, crow, cry, fry, free, three, through, crew, cue, threw

List Seven:

dry, try, tree, three, free, fray, ray, say, slay, slow

List Eight:

clay, clue, glue, grew, gray, grow, crow, cry, crew, cue

List Nine:

tree, true, drew, draw, dry, try, tray, bray, pray, play

List Ten:

slew, slee, see, say, slay, sly, lie, sigh, so, slow

CCV All Consonant sounds
s, r, l blends
Sentences for Reading and Dictation Lists on to Ten

1. Fran likes to play with clay by the cray.

2. Stan ate a slew of stew in the snow.

3. Gram can brew blue tea like a pro.

4. The flea did plea to be free from the tree.

5. Is it true that he drew a spy with one eye?

6. Throw the crow through the crew of three on the ship.

7. Try to dry the wet fly and the flea.

8. The clay crow is gray and needs some glue.

9. He can try to draw a tree on the tray.

10. He was too slow to see what flew by the crow.

CCVC | 11-20 | S Blends
Short Vowels and Long Vowels

List Eleven: p, m, t, l in s blends with long and short vowel i: *final e, -ck, FLOSS, y for long i:*
stick, still, spill, pill, pile, tile, style, smile, mile, mill

List Twelve: p, k, d, l, n in s blends with long and short vowel e *-[-ee-], [-ea-], final –ch and k:*
speech, speak, speck, sped, speed, seed, seek, sneak, sleek, leak

List Thirteen: t, n, k, g , p, l in s blends with long and short vowel a- *final e, -ck:*
stake, stack, stag, snag, snap, sap, cap, cape, scape, scale

List Fourteen: p, t, l, n, s in s blends with long and short vowel u- [-oo-], [-al-],
[-oo-], [-ou-]:
stun, spun, spoon, spool, stool, stoop, scoop, snoop, soup, soon

List Fifteen: t, v, p, k, m in s blends with long and short vowel o- *final e, [-al-] –ck:*
stove, stole, stall, stop, stock, stoke, smoke, smock, small, mall

List Sixteen: m, sh, j [dge] ch, z, s blends with short vowels a, u, and i - *-dge, -tch, [-ee-]:*
smash, smush, smudge, smidge, Smith, smitch, snitch, snatch, snazz, sneeze

List Seventeen: l, w, ch, p, f, n, t, s blends with short vowels i, e:
slim, swim, switch, swill, swell, smell, spell, spill, spiff, sniff, stiff

List Eighteen: l, t, d, j [ge] s blends with long i, a, e [ee] [-igh-], -ge, [-ee-], final e:
slight, slate, Slade, spade, speed, steed, steel, stale, state, stage

List Nineteen: n, t, l, p s blends with long a, o, u:
snub, snob, snot, slot, slat, slap, slop, stop, snop, snap

List Twenty: t, p, k, n, w, s blends with long e [ee], i, o - *[-ea-], [-ee-], final e, y for long i:*
steam, steep, sleep, slope, scope, skype, snipe, swipe, sweep, swap

CCVC S Blends
Short Vowels and Long Vowels
Lists Eleven to Twenty Reading Page

List Eleven:

stick, still, spill, pill, pile, tile, style, smile, mile, mill

List Twelve:

speech, speak, speck, sped, speed, seed, seek, sneak, sleek, leak

List Thirteen:

stake, stack, stag, snag, snap, sap, cap, cape, scape, scale

List Fourteen:

stun, spun, spoon, spool, stool, stoop, scoop, snoop, soup, soon

List Fifteen:

stove, stole, stall, stop, stock, stoke, smoke, smock, small, mall

List Sixteen:

smash, smush, smudge, smidge, Smith, smitch, snitch, snatch, snazz, sneeze

List Seventeen:

slim, swim, switch, swill, swell, smell, spell, spill, spiff, sniff

List Eighteen:

slight, slate, Slade, spade, speed, steed, steel, stale, state, stage

List Nineteen:

snub, snob, snot, slot, slat, slap, slop, stop, snop, snap

List Twenty:

steam, steep, sleep, slope, scope, skype, snipe, swipe, sweep

CCVC S Blends
Short Vowels and Long Vowels
Sentences for Reading and Dictation Lists Eleven to Twenty

1. She picked up a stick and put it in a pile by the mill with a smile.

2. His sleek steed ran with speed to sneak up on the spy in the far land.

3. Put a stake on the cape and add to the stack by the scale.

4. Spoon the soup by the stoop for the snoop on the stool.

5. The smoke on the stove came from the stock in the pot.

6. Mr. Smith can sneeze with snazz and smash a smidge of the stash.

7. Slim Jim can sniff, swim, spell and swell really well.

8. His steed is slate gray like the color of a steel spade.

9. Watch the snob stop to snub the boy with snot on his face.

10. The wind will sweep the steam up the steep slope.

CCVC | 21-30 | L Blends
p, b, t, d, k, g, l, sh, s, j, m
Short Vowels and Long Vowels

List Twenty-one: f, s, t, p, d, k in L blends with short i - *-ck:*
flit, fit, sit, slit, slip, lip, lid, slid, slick, lick

List Twenty-two: p, f, b, s, d, j [dge] in L blends and short e- *FLOSS, -dge, -ck:*
pledge, ledge, fledge, fleck, bleck, bless, less, led, bled, fled

List Twenty-three: f, t, g, s, k m in L blends and short a: - *-ck, silent b:*
flat, flag, lag, sag, slag, slack, sack, Sam, slam, lamb

List Twenty-four: p, k, g, s, sh in L blends and short u: *FLOSS, -ck:*
pluck, luck, lug, plug, plum, plus, pus, fuss, fush, flush

List Twenty-five: p, g, k, t, s in L blends and short o: *-ck:*
plot, plog, log, lock, clock, cock, cog, clog, blog, bog

List Twenty-six: s, f, p, k, t, and L blends with long and short vowel I: *-ck, [-igh-]:*
slick, flick, flit, flight, light, plight, ply, sly, slight, slit

List Twenty-seven: s, p, b, f, d, m, k, sh, j [dge] in L blends with long and short vowel */e/- [-ee-], -dge:*
sleek, sleep, bleep, bleem, blem, bled, fled, flesh, fledge, sledge

List Twenty-eight: f, p, g, sh, k, m, in blends with long and short vowel /a/- finale e:
flap, flag, flash, clash, clam, claim, blame, lame, flame, fame

List Twenty-nine: p, b, m, g, k, f in /l/ blends with long and short vowel */u/- final e, [-oo-]:*
plume, bloom, bloop, gloop, glup, plup, pluck, plush, flush, flub

List Thirty: k, g, s, b, f, n, in /l/ blends with long and short vowel */o/- final e, [-oa-], -ck, [-ow-]:*
clock, clog, slog, blog, block, bloke, blown, flown, Sloan, slope

CCVC L Blends
Short Vowels and Long Vowels Lists
Lists Twenty-One to Thirty Reading Page

List Twenty-One:

flit, fit, sit, slit, slip, lip, lid, slid, slick, lick

List Twenty-two:

pledge, ledge, fledge, fleck, bleck, bless, less, led, bled, fled

List Twenty-three

flat, flag, lag, sag, slag, slack, sack, Sam, slam, lamb

List Twenty-four:

pluck, luck, lug, plug, plum, plus, pus, fuss, fush, flush

List Twenty-five:

plot, plog, log, lock, clock, cock, cog, clog, blog, bog

List Twenty-Six:

slick, flick, flit, flight, light, plight, ply, sly, slight, slit

List Twenty-Seven:

sleek, sleep, bleep, bleem, blem, bled, fled, flesh, fledge, sledge

List Twenty-Eight:

flap, flag, flash, clash, clam, claim, blame, lame, flame, fame

List Twenty-Nine:

plume, bloom, bloop, gloop, glup, plup, pluck, plush, flush, flub

List Thirty:

clock, clog, slog, blog, block, bloke, blown, flown, Sloan, slope

CCVC L Blends
Short Vowels and Long Vowels
Sentences for Reading and Dictation Lists Twenty-One to Thirty

1. The bird flit and slid on the slick lid.

2. I pledge to stay on the ledge to bless the ones who fled.

3. The flat flag will sag so give it some slack to blow in the wind.

4. Pluck a plum from the tree and use it to plug the hole.

5. The cock will plod to the log and crow when the clock strikes three.

6. The man on the flight saw a slight flick of light through the slit in the cloud.
7. The sleek sheep fled and tried to bleat in his sleep.

8. The glam clams moved with a flash before they could clash with the slugs.

9. Pluck the plume of the bloom for the gloop.

10. Sloan will clog and slog up the slope before the bloke can make the clock chime.

CCVC | 31-40 | R Blends
Short Vowels and Long Vowels

List Thirty-One: b, t, g, f, p, l, d, in r blends short vowel i – *FLOSS:*
Brit, brig, frig, rig, trig, trip, trill, drill, drip, dip

List Thirty-Two: d, p, s, t, k in r blends with short vowel e- *FLOSS, [-ea-], [-ch for k]:*
dress, press, prep, rep, red, dread, tread, Ted, tech, trek

List Thirty-Three: b, s, k, g, in r blends with short vowel a *FLOSS:*
bass, brass, crass, crab, grab, gab, dab, drab, drag, rag

List Thirty-Four: m, f, d, g, t, k, s, in r blends short vowel u- *FLOSS, -ck:*
from, drum, drug, rug, tug, tuck, truck, truss, Russ, gruss

List Thirty-Five: k, s, d, t, p, g, f, blends short vowel o – *[-augh-]:*
cross, Ross, rod, trod, prod, pod, pog, fog, frog, fraught

List Thirty-Six: g, p, m, b, f, in r blends with long and short vowel /i/ - *final e, FLOSS:*
grip, grim, grime, prime, prim, brim, brick, brig, frig, frill

List Thirty-Seven: g, d, s, t, k, f, in r blends with long and short vowel /e/- *FLOSS, [-ea-]:*
Greg, reg, dreg, dress, press, tress, trek, wreck, wreak, freak

List Thirty-Eight: k, f, m, l, b, sh, t in r blends with long and short vowel /a/- *final e, [-ai-], -ck:*
cram, Fram, frame, frail, grail, brail, brake, brack, brash, trash

List Thirty-Nine: sh, g, b, j [dge], m, l in r blends with long and short vowel /u/- *-dge, [-oo-], [-ue-]:*
shrug, shrub, grub, grudge, grum, groom, broom, brool, cruel, cool

List Forty: d, p, m, g, f, k, b, in r blends with long and short vowel /o/- *-ck, final e, [-oa-]:*
drop, prop, prom, prog, frog, frock, brock, broke, croak, crock

CCVC R Blends
Short Vowels and Long Vowels
Lists Thirty-One to Forty Reading Page

List Thirty-One:

Brit, brig, frig, rig, trig, trip, trill, drill, drip, dip

List Thirty-Two:

dress, press, prep, rep, red, dread, tread, Ted, tech, trek

List Thirty-Three:

bass, brass, crass, crab, grab, gab, dab, drab, drag, rag

List Thirty-Four:

from, drum, drug, rug, tug, tuck, truck, truss, Russ, gruss

List Thirty-Five:

cross, Ross, rod, trod, prod, pod, pog, fog, frog, fraught

List Thirty-Six:

grip, grim, grime, prime, prim, brim, brick, brig, frig, frill

List Thirty-Seven:

Greg, reg, dreg, dress, press, tress, trek, wreck, wreak, freak

List Thirty-Eight:

cram, Fram, frame, frail, grail, braille, brake, brack, brash, trash

List Thirty-Nine:

shrug, shrub, grub, grudge, grum, groom, broom, brool, cruel, cool

List Forty:

drop, prop, prom, prog, frog, frock, brock, broke, croak, crock

CCVC R Blends
Short Vowels and Long Vowels
Sentences for Reading and Dictation for Lists Thirty-One to Forty

1. Brit got on the frig to take a trip.

2. Jen put on a red dress to tread the path on her long trek.

3. The bass swam through the brass ring by the crag.

4. Russ could hear the drum of the truck rolling on the road.

5. Ross the frog fought his way to cross the road.

6. Grip the cup to fill it to the brim with your prime punch.

7. Greg can press the dress for the girl with a long tress.

8. Fran put the grail in the trash with the frame and the brake for the bike.

9. The groom will use the broom to sweep the shrub into the cool night.

10. The croak of the frog was a prop for the play.

CCVC | 41-50 | R and L Blends
Short Vowels and Long Vowels

List Forty-One: b, p, d, f, t, in r and L blends with long /i/ and /u/- *[drop the –y to add -ed], [-igh-],*
final e:
bride, pride, dried, tried, fried, fright, bright, blight, flight, flute

List Forty-Two: b, p, t, d, r and L blends with long /i/ and /a/ - *[-ay- with –ed], final e, [-igh-], [drop the –y to add -ed]:*
blade, played, prayed, trade, tried, pride, bride, bide, bite, bright

List Forty-Three: m, t, b, f, n, b, in r and L blends with mixed long /i/, /e/ and /o/-*final e,*
[-igh-], [-oa-], [-ow-], [-ee-]:
lime, light, blight, bloat, float, flown, blown, bloat, bleat, bleed

List Forty-Four: b, m, t, d, p r and L blends with long /u/ and /oo/ *[-oo-], final e:*
bloom, boom, broom, brute, root, Ruth, truth, true, troop, droop

List Forty-Five: b, k, d, m, p, s, r, and L blends with mixed long vowels – *[-ea-], [-ee-]:*
dream, cream, creed, creep, keep, seep, sleep, bleep, blop, blob

List Forty-Six: p, d, n, t, l, k, g in r and L blends & long vowels – *final e, [-ai-], [-ea-], [-ee-]:*
prone, drone, drain, train, trail, trait, treat, greet, Crete, cleat

List Forty-Seven: f, t, g, s, p, m, in r & L blends with mixed vowels *-augh, final e,*
[-oo-]:
fraught, frog, frag, Flag, slag, slog, slug, plug, plum, plume

List Forty -Eight: g, p, d, t, s, p in L blends with mixed long and short vowels – *final e, [-ay- with –ed] [-oo-], [-ee-]:*
glade, played, plate, slate, sleet, slit, slip, slope, sloop, stoop

List Forty -Nine: b, v, t, n, in r blends with long /a/ and /o/ - *[-ai-], final e, silent w:*
brave, rave, rove, wrote, rate, trait, train, drain, drone, roan

List Fifty: d, t, b, in r blends with mixed long and short vowels – *[-ea-], [-igh-], [-ee-], [-ough-] final e:*
dread, tread, bread, breed, bride, bright, Brit, brat, brought, trot

CCVC R and L Blends
Short Vowels and Long Vowels
Lists Forty-One to Fifty Reading Page

List Forty -One:

bride, pride, dried, tried, fried, fright, bright, blight, flight, flute

List Forty -Two:

blade, played, prayed, trade, tried, pride, bride, bide, bite, bright

List Forty -Three:

lime, light, blight, bloat, float, flown, blown, bloat, bleat, bleed

List Forty-Four:

bloom, boom, broom, brute, root, Ruth, truth, true, troop, droop

List Forty -Five:

dream, cream, creed, creep, keep, seep, sleep, bleep, blop, blob

List Forty -Six:

prone, drone, drain, train, trail, trait, treat, greet, Crete, cleat

List Forty -Seven:

fraught, frog, frag, Flag, slag, slog, slug, plug, plum, plume

List Forty -Eight:

glade, played, plate, slate, sleet, slit, slip, slope, sloop, stoop

List Forty -Nine:

brave, rave, rove, wrote, rate, trait, train, drain, drone, roan

List Fifty:

dread, tread, bread, breed, bride, bright, Brit, brat, brought, trot

CCVC R and L Blends
Sentences for Reading and Dictation for lists Forty-One to Fifty

1. The bride played a bright tune on her flute with pride.

2. He will bide his time and trade his pride for a bright bride.

3. The boat did float and was blown into the limelight.

4. Ruth picked up the bloom with the broom.

5. At night Ruth did dream about true cream in her sleep.

6. The drone flew over Crete to greet the train.

7. The slug saw the frog loom near the plum.

8. He played in the glade near the slope with his slate.

9. The brave little train chugged over the drain.

10. Brit ate bread and brought some to his bright bride.

CVCC | 51-60 | R L S and Nasal Sounds

List Fifty-One One: k, w, in -pt, -lm, -st blends with short e and long i– *[doubling consonants], adding –ed, FLOSS:*
kept, wept, wiped, whipped, wit, wet, west, Wes, well, weld

List Fifty-Two Two: w, r, l, in -sp, -lt, -ld, --nd, -nt blends with short a and o - *silent w, [-al-], FLOSS, sight word 'was':*
wrap, rasp, wasp, was, wall, Walt, what, wad, wand, wind

List Fifty-Three: w, p, m, t, in -st, -ld, -lf blends with short u and long o- *FLOSS, -ed,   [-oa-] [long o with –st &–ld], {-short u as [-olf-] & [-oo-]}*
wolf, wool, pull, pulled, polled, old, mold, mode, moat, most

List Fifty-Four: p, l, s, -mp, -sp, -ps, -ft blends with short u and i:
lap, lamp, limp, lisp, lips, sips, sip, sit, sift, lift

List Fifty-Five: p, k, r, -st, -sk, -nk blends and the consonant phoneme/ng/ with short e and i:
pesk, peck, pick, pink, ink, link, rink, ring, writ, wrist

List Fifty-Six: p, l, s, -nd, -sk, -kt, -nk blends and the consonant phoneme /ng/ with short a:
act, pact, pack, lack, lad, land, sand, sank, sang, Sal

List Fifty-Seven: s, f, k, t, -lt, -ld, -nd, -st blends with short o and long o-- *[-au-], [-al-], FLOSS, [-oa-], [-ol-]:*
salt, Saul, fall, foal, fold, cold, colt coat, coast, toast

List Fifty-Eight: b, s, lt, -ld, -nd, -nt, -lk blends with short u, i, e -- *FLOSS, [-ui-]:*
bulk, bilk, bill, built, bit, bet, belt, bent, sent, send

List Fifty-Nine: sh, y, ch, -md, ld, with short i, e and long i, e- *FLOSS, -ed, [-il-], final ee, [-ie-], contraction with 'will':*
chilled, child, chimed, chide, shied, shed shelled, yelled, yield, shield

List Sixty: all sh, ch, n, y, d, in /r/ blends with diphthongs- *-or-, -ir- -ear-, -ar-:*
short, shirt, shirp, chirp, churn, yearn, yarn, yard, shard, chard

CVCC and CCVCC
Lists Fifty-One to Sixty Reading Page

List Fifty-One:

kept, wept, wiped, whipped, wit, wet, west, Wes, well, weld

List Fifty-Two:

wrap, rasp, wasp, was, wall, Walt, what, wad, wand, wind

List Fifty-Three:

wolf, wool, pull, pulled, polled, old, mold, mode, moat, most

List Fifty-Four:

lap, lamp, limp, lisp, lips, sips, sip, sit, sift, lift

List Fifty-Five:

pesk, peck, pick, pink, ink, link, rink, ring, writ, wrist

List Fifty-Six:

act, pact, pack, lack, lad, land, sand, sank, sang, Sal

List Fifty-Seven:

salt, Saul, fall, foal, fold, cold, colt coat, coast, toast

List Fifty-Eight:

bulk, bilk, bill, built, bit, bet, belt, bent, sent, send

List Fifty-Nine:

chilled, child, chimed, chide, shied, shed shelled, yelled, yield, shield

List Sixty:

short, shirt, shirp, chirp, churn, yearn, yarn, yard, shard, chard

CVCC and CCVCC
Sentences for Reading and Dictation for Lists Fifty-One to Sixty

1. She wept and wiped the wet whipped cream off her face.

2. Walt took the wand and put it in a wad of wrap.

3. The wolf pulled the old wool over his back.

4. The lump on the old man's back made him limp.

5. Pick up the pink ink pen and draw a link from one ring to the other.

6. Sal acted and sang on the land that sank in the sand.

7. He named his colt Saul because it looked like salt from the coast.

8. He built a bent hulk with the bulk of the sand that you sent.

9. The child chilled the shelled nuts while the bell chimed.

10. The short grandma can churn butter in the yard while the birds chirp.

List Sixty-One: s, l, d, with nasal blends -mp, -nd, - nk, consonant ng with short e, a, u:
send, said, sud, sup, sump, lump, lamp, lap, Lang, lank

List Sixty-Two: s, l with nasal blends -mp, -nd, - nk with short a, u, i *—silent b:*
sand, sank, sunk, sun, sum, sump, lump, limp, limb, lamb

List Sixty-Three: l, t, ch, and s blends with nasal blend -mp using short a, u, o:
lap, lamp, tamp, stamp, stump, sump, chump, champ, chomp, chop

List Sixty-Four: k, t, d, l with -rd, -rt, -rn, -rk — *using diphthongs for [-or-], [-ar-]:*
cork, corn, cord, card, cart, part, park, lark, lard, Lord

List Sixty-Five, b, f, t with -rt, -rp, -rm, -rn, -rk — *using diphthongs for [-ur-], [-er-], [-or-]:*
burp, burn, berm, firm, fir, for, fork, form, fort, port

List Sixty-Six s blends and nasal blends -sp, -nt, -nd, -ld *FLOSS, -ed, doubling consonants, -ed, FLOSS:*
spend, spent, sent, send, sand, spanned, spinned, spilled, spill, sill

List Sixty-Seven: s blends and nasal blends [-sp, -nt, -nd, -kt] in *-ed, -ck, [-oa-]:*
sacked, smacked, smoked, soaked, stoked, staked, stacked, stack, Stan, stand

List Sixty-Eight: l blends and nasal blends pl, bl, cl, nt, nd, nk
plant, planned, plank, blank, clank, clink, link, tink, think, thank

List Sixty-Nine: r, s, and nasal blends dr, sk, sp, st, nk
drank, drink, drunk, dunk, chunk, sunk, skunk, spunk, stunk, stink

List Seventy: r, s, and nasal blends shr, pr, pl, st, -nk, -nd
rink, shrink, shrank, prank, plank, lank, tank, stank, stand, sand

CVCC and CCVCC
Sixty-One to Seventy Reading Page

List Sixty-One:
send, said, sud, sup, sump, lump, lamp, lap, Lang, lank

List Sixty-Two:
sand, sank, sunk, sun, sum, sump, lump, limp, limb, lamb

List Sixty-Three
lap, lamp, tamp, stamp, stump, sump, chump, champ, chomp, chop

List Sixty-Four:
cork, corn, cord, card, cart, part, park, lark, lard, Lord

List Sixty-Five:
burp, burn, berm, firm, fir, for, fork, form, fort, port

List Sixty-Six:
spend, spent, sent, send, sand, spanned, spinned, spilled, spill, sill

List Sixty-Seven:
sacked, smacked, smoked, soaked, stoked, staked, stacked, stack, Stan, stand

List Sixty-Eight:
plant, planned, plank, blank, clank, clink, link, tink, think, thank

List Sixty-Nine:
drank, drink, drunk, dunk, chunk, sunk, skunk, spunk, stunk, stink

List Seventy:
rink, shrink, shrank, prank, plank, lank, tank, stank, stand

CVCC and CCVCC
Sentences for Reading and Dictation
Lists Sixty-One to Seventy

1. The tall, lank lad sat like a lump on the land by the sump pump.

2. The lamb sank in the sand as the sun sunk.

3. He tried to stomp out the fire made by the lamp when the champ tried to chop the stump.

4. The card shows part of a park with corn growing and a lark singing.

5. They built a fort near the port to keep the form from burning.

6. He spent more for the spilled milk than he spent for the sand by the sill.

7. Stan sacked the food and stoked the fire until it smoked.

8. I think the link between the clank and the clink is a blank plank.

9. He drank his drink until the skunk stunk.

10. The child played a prank that made the tank by the rink start to stink.

CCVC CVCC | 71-80 | R & L Blends
sh, th, ch, r-controlled vowels | Short Vowels

USE CCVCC WORKSHEET

List Seventy-One: sh, th, b, -rk, -rd, and 'ea' 'ar' 'ir' 'ough'---rk shr thr br
shirk, Shrek, shred, thread, bread, breath, broth, Roth, Ruth, truth

List Seventy-Two: ch, b, p, -rch, and ur, ir, er, 'ea' 'oa' 'ow'--- rch
church, birch perch, preach, reach, roach, row, pro, pour, porch,

List Seventy-Three: ch, j [ge], m, b, w, l, -rth, -rk, -ri, 'ar' 'er' 'ur' 'ir''or''ea' FLOSS
charge, large, Marge, merge, murk, mirth, birth, worth, were, word

List Seventy-Four: p, k, h, n, f, j [ge]. -rs, -rth, -rj and 'ur' 'our' 'or' 'ear' --- rs, -rth   -rge
purse, curse, course, horse, Norse, north, nor, for, forge, George,

List Seventy-Five: b, ch, h, z, -ls [lz] ers [rz]
belch, bell, bells, bills, bill, chill, chills, hills, his, hers

List Seventy-Six: p, s, f, h, m, k, -rs, 'se' 'ce' 'ea' 'ier' 'or' 'our' 'ur' 'rs'
peace, pierce, fierce, force, horse, Morse, source, course, curse, purse

List Seventy-Seven: sh, k, t, ch, j [ge] -rp, -rk, rt, tj [rge] 'ar' 'ir' shr 'ge'
sharp, shark, shirk, Shrek, sheck, shack, shat chat chart charge

List Seventy-Eight: th, m, r, t, thr, i.e.,' 'ea' 'ue' 'ough' 'oo'
thief, thieve, theme, ream, room, rue through, true, truth, Ruth

List Seventy-Nine: m, ch, p, j [ge], -rch, -rj [dge]'ar' 'or' 'ur' 'er' 'rge' 'rch'
mar, March, arch, parch, porch, poor, purr, purge, merge, urge,

List Eighty: th, r, sh, p, -thr, - shr, 'ow' 'ough' 'ew'
throb, rob, robe, row, throw, through, shrew, shrewd, prude, rude

CCVC CVCC R and L Blends
R controlled vowels |Short Vowels
Lists Seventy--One to Eighty Reading Page sh, th, ch

List Seventy-One:

shirk, Shrek, shred, thread, bread, breath, broth, Roth, Ruth, truth

List Seventy-Two:

church, birch perch, preach, reach, roach, row, pro, porch, torch

List Seventy-Three:

charge, large, Marge, merge, murk, mirth, birth, worth, were, well

List Seventy-Four:

purse, curse, course, Horse, Norse, north, nor, for, forge, George

List Seventy-Five:

belch, bell, bells, bills, pill, chill, chills, hills, his, her

List Seventy-Six:

peace, pierce, fierce, force, horse, Morse, source, course, curse, purse

List Seventy-Seven:

sharp, shark, shirk, Shrek, sheck, shack, shat chat chart charge

List Seventy-Eight:

thief, thieve, theme, ream, room, rue through, true, truth, Ruth,

List Seventy-Nine:

mar, March, arch, parch, porch, poor, purr, purge, merge, urge

List Eighty:
throb, rob, robe, row, throw, through, shrew, shrewd, prude, rude

CVCC and CCVCC
Sentences for Reading and Dictation Lists Seventy-One to Eighty

1. Shrek took a breath and put the thread through the cloth.

2. I saw a torch by the birch tree near the church.

3. Marge put a charge on her card for the large chair for her porch.

4. George took a course to learn how to ride a horse.

5. She put bills and pills in her purse.

6. The shrill and fierce curse pierced the peace.

7. The shark had sharp teeth.

8. The thief told the truth to Ruth.

9. We saw the arch in March before we had the urge to put up a porch.

10. The shrewd man war rude, no prude and a thief.

CCVC CVCC | 81-90 | Nasal Blends
r, l, mp, nd, nt, nk, ft, ng, -ed ending | long &short vowels

USE CCVCC WORKSHEET

List Eighty-One: l, r, mp, k, short vowel u and a
cramp, ramp, ram, lamb, clam, clamp, lamp, lump, plump, plum

List Eighty -Two: sp , st, l , nt, nd and short a and e
spent, spend, send, sand, stand, tanned, land, l end, lent, rent

List Eighty -Three: fr, t, cr, md, mp, med
frame, framed, famed, fame, tame, tam, tamp, ramp, ram, cram

List Eighty Four: cr, cl, mp, short a , u, o
cramp, camp, clamp, clam, lam, sam, sum, sump, pump, pomp

List Eighty -Five: st, sl, pl, nk, nt short a and i
rank, sank, stank, stink, sink, slink, slank, plank, plant, slant

List Eighty -Six: ft, , short I, e, o; ough, augh, -ed ending
lift, left, let, lot, loft, soft, sought, caught, cough, coughed

List Eighty Seven: nt, nd, h, f, r, t, l short e, u, a , long I, -ed ending – doubling consonants
hunt, runt, rent, tent, tend, lend, lined, find, fend, fanned

List Eighty Eight: tr, short i, e, u; -ed ending – doubling consonants
trimmed, rimmed, rim, hymn, hem, hemmed, hummed, hum

List Eighty -Nine: st, sl, cl, ng, nk, shot u, I, a; doubling consonants & -ed ending
stun, stunned, stunk, stink, sink, slink, sling, cling, clank, clink

List Ninety: th, t, w, nk, ng, lk, -short i, a, -al, ed ending
thank, tank, tang, ting, thing, wing, wink, wick, walk, walked

CVCC and CCVCC
Eighty-One to Ninety Reading Page

List Eighty-One:
cramp, ramp, ram, lamb, clam, clamp, lamp, lump, plump, plum

List Eighty -Two:
spent, spend, send, sand, stand, tanned, land, l end, lent, rent

List Eighty -Three:
frame, framed, famed, fame, tame, tam, tamp, ramp, ram, cram

List Eighty Four
cramp, camp, clamp, clam, lam, sam, sum, sump, pump, pomp

List Eighty -Five:
rank, sank, stank, stink, sink, slink, slank, plank, plant, slant

List Eighty -Six:
lift, left, let, lot, loft, soft, sought, caught, cough, coughed

List Eighty Seven:
hunt, runt, rent, tent, tend, lend, lined, find, fend, fanned

List Eighty Eight:
trimmed, rimmed, rim, hymn, hem, hemmed, hummed, hum

List Eighty -Nine:
stun, stunned, stunk, stink, sink, slink, sling, cling, clank, clink

List Ninety:
thank, tank, tang, ting, thing, wing, wink, wick, walk, walked

CVCC and CCVCC

Sentences for Reading and Dictation Lists Eighty-One to Ninety

1. The plump clam had a cramp in his claw.

2. If you lend the rent to the man, he may spend it for a clamp instead.

3. The famed ramp is framed for all to see.

4. Sam came in with much pomp until he could not fix the sump pump.

5. The plant sat on the plank until the slant of the sinking boat tipped it over.

6. The girl caught a bad cough and left the loft.

7. He paid rent for the tent and fanned the flame before he left for the hunt.

8. She trimmed the hem before she hemmed the skirt.

9. The stunned skunk tried to slink away.

10. I think the ting in the tank is nothing to wink at.

CHAPTER 8

BUILDING FLUENCY and ACCURACY
in READING and SPELLING

PHONICS

Understanding Phonics Rules for Building Words is critical for growth in spelling accuracy and reading unknown words. There are many well written books dedicated to the topic of phonics. In schools today, phonic instruction is emphasized in kindergarten and elementary school more than it was a few years ago. Hence, this chapter will be an overview of the phonic rules presented in the word lists rather than an in-depth study.

Point 1 The Short Vowel Rules! The short vowel tone directs consonant letter patterns that follow, but many people cannot hear the difference between the short vowel tones. When one cannot hear or "process" differences between the long and short vowel tones, it is impossible to understand the rules of phonics.

a. The 'final e' on the end of a word, in most cases, will not follow a short vowel.
   i.e., dim vs. dime | pet vs. Pete |can vs. cane |cut vs. cute | pop vs. pope

b. Words ending in /l/, /f/, and /s/ occur after a short vowel tone, have two letters 'll' 'ff' and 'ss'
   Mill | cuff | miss   but after the long vowel, the letters do not double   mile | mice | life

c. The '-ck', -tch, and –dge patterns always follow a short vowel, never a long vowel.
   i.e. luck vs. Luke | fill vs. file | etch vs. each | tack vs. take |
   ledge | dodge | wage | huge

d. The spelling of the second syllable when endings are added is dependent upon the vowel tone in the preceding syllable.

When a second syllable ending, such as -ing, -ed, -ful, -est, -er, etc. is added to a one syllable word, the vowel sound in the first syllable could be changed by adding the second syllable. How? The first syllable is either 'open' or 'closed' depending upon the last letter in the syllable.

So, when writing the word, it is important to "hear" the tone of the vowel in the first syllable before adding the ending. I tell students to listen for the sound of a letter name in the first syllable [or word without the ending]. If the vowel tone sounds like it is speaking the name of a letter, then the syllable is either

- an open syllable
- has a vowel spelled with two letters
- or is a one-syllable word ending with an 'e'

For example, the words I **| a | go | she| me |,** end with vowel letters and long vowel sounds. They are open syllable words. In two syllable words, the same rule applies. As you look at the words below, notice that the last letter in the first syllable of an OPEN syllable is a vowel letter. Notice that the last letter in a CLOSED syllable is a consonant. I tell the students that the vowel in a CLOSED syllable is turned off, so it cannot "speak" the letter name, but the OPEN syllable is turned on and can "speak" the letter name.

OPEN: di – ner | fi -ling | cra – dle | ho – ping

CLOSED: din –ner | fil -ling | lit – tle | hop –ping

The short vowel tones will have a consonant after the vowel tone in the first syllable.

For the student to understand this rule, they MUST HEAR the vowel tone differences or the rule will make no sense to them. To hear the differences between vowel tones, they must be able to separate [segment] the vowel tone from the surrounding sounds [or phonemes] AND discriminate between tones [hear the differences between them], which is difficult for students with auditory processing disorders and/or dyslexia.

A poster and phonic cards contrasting the long and short vowel phonic rules can be found in Chapter 11.

SPELLING TWO-SYLLABLE WORDS

Spelling Two-Syllable Words After working through the lessons covered in Chapters 4 and 5 using the word lists in Chapters 6 and 7, your student is now ready to tackle two syllable words and word endings. (Educators often refer to the use of endings on words as "morphology.") For some students, teaching morphology will not even be necessary! Children who command excellent speech and use of language, use word endings when speaking correctly. Therefore, once they have skills for sequencing and speaking the phonemes as they write, matching letters and sounds, understand the basic phonic rules , then adding the endings to words will naturally flow. If they have developed reading fluency using repeated reading and phrasing, progress will gain even more momentum moving forward.

However, there will be a few students needing help with longer words. It would be fantastic if I could locate enough words to chain two syllable words as you saw for one syllable words in Chapters 6 and 7, but it just does not work that way. So, minimal pairs are used at first and gradually and other kinds of add two syllable words are added when the student can identify the differences between the minimal pairs. Wipe off boards and dry erase markers are fun for the students when we work on these. If you are working virtually with a student, then annotate function and a blank word doc or virtual white board will work well as well.

Step 1: Using a wipe off board or virtual screen with annotate or shared screen control turned on, show the student words with open syllables

Such as "I" "me" "a" "go" etc. A longer list is included at the end of this section.

Step 2: Add a consonant to the end of each word and talk about how the added letter changed the word and the vowel tone.

Step 3: Show two words that are the same except one has a double consonant in the middle:

super vs. supper | diner vs. dinner

Discuss how syllables 'usually' begin with a consonant letter. Therefore, the second syllable will 'steal' a consonant from the end of the first syllable. So, to stop the vowel sound from changing, the first syllable must add another letter.

Practice writing words with open and closed syllables and adding word endings to words on the wipe off boards or virtual screen. As the teacher, be sure to write and show your words to your student for comparison. Be sure to continue saying sounds [not letter names] simultaneously as you are writing as practiced during earlier lessons.

Open and Closed Syllables

a	am	at	be	bet	Ben	bell	go	got	God
me	met	men	mess	by	bit			we	wet	wed
I	it	ill		in	so	sop	sock	she	shell	shed
my	mill	miss		no	not	net		he	hem	hen
			Hi	hit	hip					

MINIMAL PAIR OPEN/CLOSED TWO SYLLABLE WORDS ENDING WITH SUFFIX

baker	hoper	hoping	odor
backer	hopper	hopping	odder
biter	hummer	filing	pacer
bitter	humor	filling	passer
hater	later	miler	planer
hatter	latter	miller	planner
primer	siting	rater	rider
primmer	sitting	ratter	ridder
riper	rooter	ruder	sniper
ripper	rotter	rudder	snipper
planer	planner	sniper	snipped
liked	licked	tiler	tiller
baked	backed	taping	tapping
typing	tipping	tiler	tiller
hoped	hopped	odor	odder
baked	backed	biker	bicker
super	supper	diner	dinner
lighter	litter	smoking	smocking

Note: A minimal pair is two words that are nearly identical except for one sound difference. In this case the sound is the vowel sound in the first syllable, which we know changes the letters used when adding the second syllable.

TWO SYLLABLE WORDS WITH -LE

title	huddle	staple
tittle	middle	scruple
cable	muddle	rumple
cobble	noodle	pimple
gable	paddle	triple [exception]
gobble	poodle	grapple
ruble	puddle	simple
rubble	riddle	temple
rifle	waddle	trample
riffle	ruffle	battle
Bible	raffle	little
table	scuffle	bottle
fable	baffle	cattle
stable	shuffle	brittle
nibble	waffle	kettle
noble	buckle	settle
pebble	chuckle	rattle
bubble	freckle	shuttle
dribble	pickle	startle
grumble	sparkle	mantle
humble	speckle	tattle
bumble	sprinkle	whittle
jumble	tackle	dazzle
crumble	tickle	drizzle
cradle	wrinkle	puzzle
idle	circle	cattle
sidle	cycle	jungle
fiddle	uncle	usable
cuddle	apple	gamble
kindle	cripple	
saddle	maple	
bridle	ripple	

DOUBLING CONSONANT WORDS WITH SUFFIX

cutest	bidding	falling	muting
dullest	billing	fanning	nagging
fattest	being	fiddling	nesting
fastest	biting	finding	netting
finest	blaming	filming	pacing
fullest	blaring	fishing	padding
fittest	bleeding	fining	passing
greenest	blessing	firing	patting
hottest	blinking	flagging	padding
hugest	bridging	flapping	paving
latest	bringing	flipping	piling
nicest	browsing	flitting	piping
oddest	browning	frying	pitting
oldest	brushing	fraying	planning
rarest	bucking	fuming	poking
richest	building	fussing	posing
rudest	clutching	grilling	popping
safest	coaching	grazing	pricing
slimmest	coding	hitting	quitting
stiffest	combining	hissing	racing
purest	costing	hogging	raging
tallest	cramping	icing	rating
truest	craving	jamming	rattling
wettest	drumming	jogging	ribbing
widest	ducking	joking	ripping
wisest	dumping	keeping	rigging
bagging	dropping	lapping	roping
baking	edging	lagging	roving
batting	ending	laying	ruling
bathing	etching	letting	running
bedding	facing	liking	saving
begging	fading	mapping	sagging
betting	faking	musing	selling

REPEATED READING

Repeated Reading Is exactly what it states – reading the same page repeatedly. In Chapter 5 repeated reading was suggested briefly with research cited. The five stories provided for assessment are also appropriate for repeated reading exercises.

In my experience, repeated reading is to reading what piano practice is to a musician, shooting hoops is to the basketball player and tossing the football is to the football player. It is what we do to get better at the skill of reading. It is what we do to build reading speed and accuracy. In Chapter 11 you will find five leveled stories and a chart for documenting your students' reading fluency. This activity should take no more than 15 minutes a day AT THE MOST! I cannot emphasize this enough:

Parents: If you and your child have time to run to sports practice and club events several days a week, why would you not have 15 minutes 3-4 times a week to practice the skill of reading? Is reading not of equal importance?

Teachers: I often hear that time does not allow for individual attention to reading fluency development using repeated reading because a certain number of minutes must be assigned to each subject every week and all the time in school day has been assigned to mandatory subjects. However, when the student cannot read the assignments and textbooks in the classroom, is it better to drag out the process of developing reading rate and accuracy [a.k.a. reading fluency], while the student struggles through all the subject areas? Or would it be better to sideline a subject area for a semester to improve reading fluency so the tasks in all the subject areas are accomplished with greater ease and efficiency? If government standards are the issue, perhaps the standards and policies need to be reviewed and modified.

READING

1. Have the student orally read a passage on their current reading level for one minute. Note the words missed. If your student struggles with a word as they read [silently count to 5], then say it for them.
2. Review the words missed with the student.
3. Read the same passage a second time for one minute following the same pattern as in 1 and 2.
4. Read the same passage a third time for one minute following the same pattern as in 1 and 2.
5. Record the best score on the student chart. Have the student color in the graph to reflect their performance each day.
6. When a child is reading a passage at 100 words per minute, go to the next area of the story that has not yet been read. Do the same pattern again.
7. When a child completes a story, go to the next level of story, and start all over. Gradually your child will increase reading rate and accuracy to grade level.

PHRASING

Phrasing is another area where students often struggle. Children with fluent speech but poor reading fluency .will often 'throttle down' and have difficulty knowing when and where to breathe when they are reading. Instead, they stop to breathe in the middle of phrases or try to race through to a period before taking a breath. Along the way they also stop to figure words. Is it any wonder they do not remember or understand what they have read? To change this habit, **when practicing their reading, they need to read out-loud**. While I would never suggest they do this in front of a group of their peers [or even one other peer], when they are alone with their parent or tutor, it must be done. As their teacher, you can model where to breathe and correct phrasing, you can give them guidance and feedback, and you can read simultaneously with them. Here is the process I follow to teach phrasing:

Day 1

1. Select an easy level passage [but be sure there are sentences containing phrases that tell how, when, where or why within the passage] of only 50 to 100 words. Choose something they have read before, but it was 'choppy.' The stories in this book are appropriate to use.
2. Use a pencil to lightly mark between phrases at those places where a pause or breath should occur.
3. Read it out loud to model.
4. Read it in chorus with the student.
5. Student read it alone.

Day 2 Use the passage read the day before unless the student achieved 80 words per minute 95% accuracy. If they did select another easy level passage of only 50 to 100 words they have read choppily before.

1. But first have the student read yesterday's passage in chorus.
2. Then read it again alone.
3. Introduce the new passage – again use a pencil to lightly mark between phrases at those places where a breath should be taken.
4. Read it out loud to model.
5. Read it in chorus with the student.
6. Student read it alone.

Day 3 Select another easy level passage of only 50 to 100 words they have read choppily before.

1. Today ask the student to read the first two passages using their phrasing.
2. Ask them to try a new [unmarked] passage alone.
3. If they do well, begin to use this strategy during repeated reading. Remind them to use their phrasing.
4. If more practice is needed, then continue as in Day 1 and 2 until phrasing practice is no longer needed.

CHAPTER 9

READING AND SPELLING FOR

MUTLIPLE SYLLABLE WORDS WITH SUFFIXES
Introduction

In the mid to late 1990's Dr. Nancy Lewkowicz, author of Word Workout and The Word Workshop , spoke at a dyslexia conference in Cincinnati. Her message was amazing, and I immediately began using her ideas to teach children how to hear, read and spell syllables in multiple syllable words. However, with younger children and limited time, it was soon apparent that changes in the way Dr. Lewkowicz's strategies were presented would need to be made.

This chapter outlines my variation on Dr. Lewkowicz's ideas so that children as early as 4th grade could apply the concept of suffix identification to finding syllables and syllable stress in words. This approach is quite workable for virtual learning using annotation and white boards, or in face to face lessons using wipe off boards and worksheets.

The basic idea uses backward chaining. Backward chaining means that you look at the last syllable first, then work backwards to the beginning of the word. Now this very idea seems counter intuitive when working with someone having dyslexia, who struggles with seeing the words in sequence on the page in the first place! However, I have found that it DOES work!

One of the main obstacles to multiple syllable word reading and writing is that there is always an unstressed vowel, and on the surface, there appears to be no pattern for predicting just where the unstressed vowel will appear in any given word. However, Dr. Lewkowicz discovered the pattern and shared that information in her presentation and book.

The pattern is based upon the final suffix. I have also found that many suffixes share the same letter patterns and are built' off just two letters and the 'uh' sound. Let's begin with how the most common suffixes are built.

First, we have the unstressed vowel or what is called 'schwa [pronounced /uh/]' sound on the end of a word. Think of the short vowel /u/ sound. Have you ever said or done something you regretted and said to yourself 'Duh!" Did I really say that out loud? I tell students that the 'schwa' sound is what the vowel says when it hides from embarrassment— "uh"

.

The ENDINGS -a | -o

Words like comma and coma end with the schwa sound. We then talk about several words ending with 'a' and sounding like /u/. 'o' will sound like the long o or long u.[*Meaning:-a common on feminine names and to mark plural in Greek | -o 'on' or 'of'.*]

banana	villa	camera	bandana	micro
hula	mica	alpha	magma	
circa	cola	tuna	oregano	
tuba	coma	jumbo	yucca	
comma	limbo	gala	drama	

ENDINGS -an |- on
Next the letter 'n' is added to the 'a' and the 'o' to form 'an' and 'on' with both sounding the same--- /u/ +/n./

[Meaning: relates meaning of the word to a person. -on forms a word into a noun.]

lemon	ocean	button	human
orphan	beacon	freshman	mailman
bacon	organ	apron	beckon

ENDINGS – al | -ol

Next, we add the letter 'l' to the vowels 'a' and 'o' as in 'metal' and 'idol.' *[mean 'kind of ' or 'pertaining*

lemon	ocean	button	human
orphan	beacon	freshman	mailman
bacon	organ	apron	beckon

ENDINGS –ia | -io

Next, we will add the letter 'i' having the long /ee/ sound right before the schwa forming 'ia' as in the name 'Julia' and /o/ as in 'trio.' *[used in names of diseases, medical terms, countries.]*

radio	anemia	hysteria	India
bacteria	insignia	mania	cafeteria
insomnia	zinnia	criteria	magnolia
virginia	dyslexia	mania	tibia
trivia	suburbia	Gloria	forsythia
phobia	media	hernia	tilapia

ENDINGS –ian | ion

Next, we add the letter 'n' to this combination. This produces 'ian' and 'ion' for /ee/+/un/.
Forms nouns from actions or adjectives |' related to 'or 'like']

amphibian	minion	bullion
median	onion	million
guardian	dominion	union

ENDINGS – tia |-sia | -cia | -tio

We add the letters 't' 's' or 'c' to produce '-tia' 'sia' or 'cia.' The combination sounds like /sh/+/u/ and
'tio' sounds like /sh/ + /o/ [long o]. *[Forms abstract nouns from verbs. -sia means 'state of.']*

inertia	dementia	amnesia
ambrosia	magnesia	ratio
acacia	minutia	militia
facia		

ENDINGS –tial | -cial

We add the letter 'l' to the end of this suffix to create '-tial' and 'cial.' Again the /sh/ + /u/ +/l/
phonemes combine to make this suffix. *[Means' relating' or 'pertaining to']*

special	social	artificial
commercial	facial	official
glacial	crucial	initial
partial	spatial	potential

ENDINGS –ous | -tious |-cious

' Next we are adding 'ous' [/us/] and 'ci' or 'ti' [/sh/ + /us/] to make -cious' and '-tious'   *[Means '*

repetitious	fictitious	superstitious
atrocious	conscious	delicious
gracious	luscious	precious
ambitious	cautious	nutritious

ENDINGS –tion | -sion | -cion | -tian | -sian | -cian

Next, we will add the letters 'an' and 'on' to the 'ti' 'ci' and 'si' [/sh/] to form 'tion' 'sion' and 'cion' or
/sh/+/un/. *[Turns action or adjective into noun.]*

addition	admission	attention
collision	compassion	confession
concussion	notion	affection
nation	emotion	suspicion

The - tion-, sion, and - cion or - tian, -sian, -cian combinations are frequently found in elementary level reading. This is one of the first groups of endings following the backward chaining pattern for unstressed syllables we will teach. The first syllable before the ending will be the stressed syllable and the second syllable back from the ending will be the unstressed syllable. The stressed/unstressed pattern backwards repeats for all remaining syllables. More on this later in the Chapter.

ENDINGS –ent | -ence | - ent
Next, we add the 'ent' and 'ence' endings for the /uh/ +/nt/ or /uh/+/ns/
[Means to cause, promote or do| -ence means to 'withdraw from' or 'absence of']

accent	recent	content
cement	fragment	figment
indent	garment	adjustment
adjacent	allotment	

ENDINGS -ient | -ience
Next, we add the /ee/ sound using the letter 'i' before the endings -ent and -ence to form the /ee/+ /uh/

lenient	nutrient	resilient
audience	convenience	ambience
orient		

MORE ENDINGS
There are several more endings that are not built from the components listed here, but the endings do follow the stressed and unstressed patterns related to backward chaining of syllables from the endings.

-y   [as in /ee/ [happy] [*Means 'inclined to']*

-fy   [amplify] *[Means 'to make' or 'cause to be'*

-ate   [originate] *[Means 'having appearance of'*

-ture   [temperature] *[Added to verb to form a noun*

-sive   [excessive] *[expresses 'tendency to']*

-ic   [magic] *[Means 'have characteristics of']*

-ize   [organize] *[Means 'to make']*

-tory [dormitory] *['to make a place']*

-ist   [scientist] *['person who practices or holds beliefs of']*

-ism   [autism] *[Means 'state or condition']*

-ary   [dictionary] *[Makes adjective a noun or receptacle]*

-ory   [category] *[Forms a noun that is a place]*

-acy   [democracy] *[Makes adjective a noun*

BEFORE WE LOOK AT THE RULES FOR EACH ENDING, GUIDELINES FOR USING ENDINGS TO READ MULTIPLE SYLLABLE WORDS

- Stressed syllable vowels sound like short vowel sounds with a few exceptions listed below.
- Unstressed syllable vowels sound like 'uh' with a few exceptions listed below.
- There can only be one vowel sound in a syllable.
- When an ending is added to a word that is already a word with an ending, the stress will follow the pattern for the ending of the 'already a word' part THEN the final ending formed by adding another ending is used. This will not make sense now, but once you see the rules, it will.

Examples: cap *i* tal and cap *i* tal ist

          2 1   1 2 *1*

- Usually syllables begin with a consonant, but the unstressed vowel will often stand alone. Will this affect your ability to find the stressed and unstressed syllable to read the word? No. Classroom teachers often teach that every syllable begins with a consonant, but in this system, that is not the case. Therefore, do not get caught up in this point. The purpose of the exercise is to be able to read the words and spell them.

Examples: hes *i* tate   *au* thor *i* ty   ec *o* nom *i* cal

      2 1   2 1 2   2 1 2 1

- A word about the spelling : The vowel letter in the unstressed syllable must be remembered when writing, since all unstressed vowels will sound like 'uh' with only a few exceptions noted below. However, once you are speaking the syllables and sounds within the syllables in your mind as you write, you will see a significant improvement in your spelling and find fewer issues with spell check on your computer, as your approximate spellings will more closely resemble the word you are writing.
- The letters 'ir' 'ur' and 'er' will not be separated. This is a vowel controlled by /r/ and is only one sound. The /r/ sound paired with vowels will give more emphasis to the unstressed syllable, but it will not be the stressed syllable unless otherwise positioned within the syllable sequence, as determined by the words' endings, to be the stressed syllable.
- Vowel combinations [diagraphs- ai | oa | etc.] will be long and will not be separated but count as one sound. You will notice that digraphs are seen with less frequency in words having 3 or more syllables.

As with all patterns in the English language, there will be that occasional exception when the word just does not follow the rule. This is often related to the word's origin from another language. I have included a few of these words in the worksheets and noted them with a * in the answer sheets found in Chapter 11.

FIVE RULES FOR FINDING STRESSED AND UNSTRESSED SYLLABLES

1. When you see the endings

   -sive | -tion |- sion | -tian |-sian |- cian |-ic. | -tia | -cia | -sia | -cious

   the **first syllable before the ending** is stressed. The vowel will have the short vowel tone.

   Some vowel exception patterns for these endings:
   When the letters ' a,' 'o,' or 'e' appear right before an ending, there is a possibility that the vowel will be long.

   Examples: *ex* |plo| sion   *com* |ple| tion |in| *di* |ca| *tion*

           2   1   2   1   1 2 1

   See videos at
       https://youtu.be/6aDNo4J2NvU
       https://youtu.be/FEJgh2KwKZg

2. When you see the endings.

   -y | -fy | -ate| -ize | -tude| -ist |-ism | -acy |-ary | -tory the **second syllable before the ending** is stressed.

   Regions of the country have different dialects. In most dialects, when the letter 'i' appears right before the ending, although the syllable is not stressed, the 'i' may be short.

   Example: |al| *ti* tude |at| *ti* *tude*

           2 1   2 1

   The letter **'u' is long** when there is only one consonant between the letter 'u' and the vowel in the next syllable. This means the syllable ending with 'u' as an open syllable.

   When there are two consonants between the letter 'u' and the vowel in the next syllable, the 'u' will be short.

   Examples: |cus| *to* dy   u |til| *i* ty

           2   1   2   1 1

3. Syllable stress, in the rest of the endings, is determined by the number of consonants between the <u>vowel in the ending</u> and the vowel in <u>the first syllable before the ending</u>.

-al | -ous |-an | -ent | -ence | -tive | -ly | -ness | -ize| -ist | -able |-ible| -ture
   - If there are **two consonants between the vowels**, the **first syllable back** is stressed.
   - If there is **one consonant between the vowels**, the **second syllable back** is stressed.
   - When the letter 'i' appears just before one of the endings listed, and there is no 't' 's' or 'c' in front, [-ial,- ion,- ian, - ient ,-ience, -ious] the ' i ' is a second vowel sound and is the long 'e' sound.

Examples: ex per i ence | on i on | me di al | re sil i ent

me di an | cur i ous

Since the 'i' is a separate vowel sound, although considered to be one suffix for meaning purposes, it will act as a separate syllable when finding the stressed and unstressed syllable for pronunciation purposes.

4. Remember that there can only be one vowel sound in any syllable. Therefore, when an ending Iis prefaced with the 'i' , the 'i' takes the long 'e' sound.
The suffix itself becomes two syllables and the 'i' is counted as one syllable before the ending when finding the stressed and unstressed syllables.

5. When a word is already a word and has a suffix on it,

Examples: cap i tal -- has the -al ending and you want to add another ending.

2   1

There is one consonant between -al and the 'i' so the number 2 is stressed.

Examples: cap i tal ism -- underline both endings.

2   1

Follow the rule for the first ending to find the stressed syllable.   In this word there is only one consonant between the vowel in the ending and the vowel before the ending. This means the stressed syllable will be the second syllable back before the ending. 'cap' is stressed.

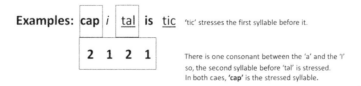

Examples: cap i tal is tic   'tic' stresses the first syllable before it.

2   1   2   1   There is one consonant between the 'a' and the 'I'
so, the second syllable before 'tal' is stressed.
In both caes, **'cap'** is the stressed syllable.

THE MULTIPLE SYLLABLE WORD LESSON

Step 1: <u>Introduce the concept of endings on words</u>. Discuss how endings change the meanings of words but reserve this aspect to a minimum amount of time. The goal is to improve the reading fluency and spelling accuracy. Vocabulary can be taught later.

The first lesson will be about the idea that words have a rhythm.
- Syllables bounce with an on/off rhythm.
- The vowel in each syllable is either 'turned on ' or 'turned off.'
- Each syllable can only have one vowel sound.

Practice ***listening*** to the rhythm of words. We are ***not looking*** at words at this point. This is a good time to read poetry to the students.

For making the rhythm visual, use your flat marbles or squares of paper, touch or move the objects up and down to show the 'bounce' of the stress on the syllable. Use words with three or more syllables and exaggerate the stress as you speak the words.

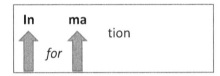

Step 2: ***Show the students a set of words ending with -tion***. This is one of the most common multiple syllable words elementary students encounter in text. Talk about how the letters -ti sound like /sh/ just like 'ch' together do not sound like /s/+/h/ or /k/ + /h/, the letters 't' and 'i' have a new sound too, when they are put together on the ends of words.

Step 3: ***Write a 3 syllable, and a 4-syllable word ending*** in -tion on your whiteboard or virtual screen. Underline the -tion ending.

Find the first vowel before the ending. If there is a blend before the vowel, keep those letters together with the vowel.

Draw a box around the syllable. Tell the student this is a stressed syllable; the vowel gets to make a sound. If there are consonants between the vowel and the 'tion,' the vowel says its short sound. If there is a letter 'a', 'o' or 'e' right before the 'tion' the vowel says its name. If it is an 'i,' it says its short sound. Avoid words containing the letter 'u' for now.

In	for	ma	tion		ep	i	dem	ic
1		2	1		1	2	1	

Next write three multiple syllable words ending with -tion on the student's white board or on the screen if you are in 'virtual' learning, and have the student underline the ending and draw a box around the stressed syllables. If you are using white boards, you will also have a whiteboard and write the words [hidden from the student]. After they mark the word, show yours to them so they can compare your work to theirs. On virtual boards wait until they are finished, and then write the same words as they watch and compare their answers.

Step 4: Give them a worksheet [see worksheets at the end of this Chapter] of words to mark and read to you or if you are on a virtual screen, use a camera to project the worksheet on to the computer's virtual screen or scan the worksheet into your computer for your personal use only with your students.

Step 5: Finally, dictate 5 words for them to write. Remind them to say one syllable at a time and each sound in each syllable as they write.

On the following pages you will find:

WORD LISTS FOR MULTIPLE SYLLABLE WORD WORKSHEETS

FOR VIRTUAL LEARNERS AND IN-PERSON LEARNERS

ARE FOUND ON THE FOLLOWING PAGES IN THE REMAINDER OF THIS CHAPTER

Answers are in Chapter 11

Worksheet 1 -tion

action   adoption
                   2   1

notion   production

caption   construction

fiction   affection

fraction   infection

Worksheet 2 -ation |-ition |-etion |-otion
Stress is on the first syllable before the ending and every other syllable moving back to the first syllable in the word.

completion

devotion

secretion

commotion

explosion

dictation

emotion

fixation

position

sensation

foundation   temptation

location   motivation

migration   devastation

condition   activation

tradition   litigation

subtraction   deposition

mitigation	partition
vacation	confiscation
desperation	competition
composition	petition
admiration	rendition
motivation	disposition

Worksheet 3 -tious | -cious

Stress is on the first syllable before the ending and every other syllable moving back to the first syllable in the word.

vicious	ambitious
infectious	superstitious
fictitious	rambunctious
nutritious	expeditious
repetitious	infectious

contentious	conscious
vexatious	judicious
facetious	gracious
pretentious	luscious
delicious	ferocious

Worksheet 4 -ic| -sia| -cia| -tia

Stress is on the first syllable before the ending and every other syllable moving back to the first syllable in the word.

majestic

Antarctic

academic

Pacific

allergic

Atlantic

analytic

epidemic

anesthetic

antiseptic

erratic characteristic

authentic democratic

botanic diplomatic

ceramic dramatic

capitalistic elastic

economic	fanatic
domestic	fantastic
electronic	pessimistic
emphatic	harmonic
pandemic	historic

magic

mechanic

melodic

catastrophic

optimistic

artistic

paralytic

inertia

acacia

ambrosia

anesthesia

fantasia

Worksheet 5 -y [not -ly] | -fy | -ate

Stress is on SECOND syllable back from ending
Counting backwards to syllable 2

com|pany

2	1

agency

academy

ability

enemy

accessibility

activity

anatomy

adversity

authority

availability

buttery

bubbly

calamity

certify

amplify

classify

dignify

satisfy

electrify

exemplify	justify
fortify	magnify
gratify	notify
glorify	abdicate
identify	accommodate

activate

agitate

motivate

considerate

advocate

certificate

affectionate

consolidate

aggravate

decorate

Worksheet 6 -tude | -ist |-ism

Stress is on SECOND syllable back from ending
Counting backwards Syllable

gratitude   altitude

attitude   magnitude

longitude   artist

latitude   botanist

solitude   colonist

cyclist

ecologist

finalist

florist

formalist

lobbyist

internist

optimist

psychologist

stigmatism

Worksheet 7 with the letter u

All the endings so far. Watch out! There are changes between stressed syllable on one or on two. It depends on the ending.

music

ultrasonic

futuristic

ab du ction

	2	1	

public

ac cu mu la tion

	2	1		2	1	

republic

accusation

rustic

fusion

combustion	constitution
suggestion	percussion
conjunction	propulsion
congratulation	transfusion
graduation	seclusion

musician

consultation

jurisdiction

speculation

contribution

utility

malnutrition

stimulation

uniformity

fortunate

Worksheet 8 -ture

Count the consonants BETWEEN the vowel in the ending and the vowel in the first syllable back. When there are 2 consonants the FIRST syllable back is stressed. When there are NO Consonants or only ONE consonant the SECOND syllable back is stressed.   See Rule #5 count the consonants between the vowels in the ending and the first syllable before it.

picture   structure

adventure   culture

departure   subculture

furniture   temperature

Worksheet 9 -ous

Count the consonants BETWEEN the vowel in the ending and the vowel in the first syllable back.
When there are 2 consonants the FIRST syllable back is stressed. When there are NO
Consonants or only ONE consonant the SECOND syllable back is stressed.   See Rule #5 count
the consonants between the vowels in the ending and the first syllable before it.

stupendous   coniferous

anonymous   conspicuous

boisterous   famous

callous   continuous

carnivorous   dangerous

.

fabulous

generous

hazardous

jealous

joyous

enormous

luminous

tumultuous

villainous

tremendous

momentous

Worksheet 10 -ary | -ory |-acy | -tory

Count the consonants BETWEEN the vowel in the ending and the vowel in the first syllable back.
When there are 2 consonants the FIRST syllable back is stressed. When there are NO
Consonants or only ONE consonant the SECOND syllable back is stressed.   See Rule #5 count
the consonants between the vowels in the ending and the first syllable before it.

anniversary   contrary

canary   dictionary

boundary   complimentary

burglary   dignitary

contemporary   culinary

hereditary	extraordinary
customary	category
honorary	circulatory
glossary	compulsory
fragmentary	contradictory

factory

satisfactory

history

victory

introductory

accuracy

memory

candidacy

laboratory

conspiracy	advocacy
delicacy	fallacy
democracy	inaccuracy
diplomacy	literacy
privacy	theocracy

Worksheet 11   -a | -an | -o | -on

Count the consonants BETWEEN the vowel in the ending and the vowel in the first syllable back.
When there are 2 consonants the FIRST syllable back is stressed. When there are NO
Consonants or only ONE consonant the SECOND syllable back is stressed.   See Rule #5 count
the consonants between the vowels in the ending and the first syllable before it.

alfalfa   bandana

algebra   gumbo

ballerina   halo

bologna   mosquito

Worksheet 12   -an |-on | -al | -ol

Count the consonants BETWEEN the vowel in the ending and the vowel in the first syllable back.
When there are 2 consonants the FIRST syllable back is stressed. When there are NO
Consonants or only ONE consonant the SECOND syllable back is stressed. See Rule #5 count the
consonants between the vowels in the ending and the first syllable before it.

veteran   pecan

began   pelican

caravan   workman

cardigan   watchman

Amazon

apron

bacon

baton

beckon

bison

abdominal

additional

actual

alphabetical

approval

bifocal

bridal

brutal

botanical

symbol

conventional

mathematical

horizontal

phenomenal

relational

economical

Worksheet 13 -ia |-io |-ial |-ian |-ion

Count the consonants BETWEEN the vowel in the ending and the vowel in the first syllable back.
When there are 2 consonants the FIRST syllable back is stressed. When there are NO
Consonants or only ONE consonant the SECOND syllable back is stressed. See Rule #5 count the
consonants between the vowels in the ending and the first syllable before it

ammonia   trivia

bacteria   utopia

criteria   suburbia

memorabilia   sepia

magnolia   hysteria

radio	amphibian
patio	civilian
polio	comedian
studio	custodian
scenario	historian

guardian	million
librarian	billion
meridian	bullion
thespian	centurion
onion	companion

dominion	scorpion
opinion	arterial
pavilion	bacterial
union	biennial
reunion	bronchial

microbial   cranial

millennial   imperial

testimonial   memorial

territorial   radial

Worksheet 14 -tial |-cial

Count the consonants BETWEEN the vowel in the ending and the vowel in the first syllable back.
When there are 2 consonants the FIRST syllable back is stressed. When there are NO
Consonants or only ONE consonant the SECOND syllable back is stressed. See Rule #5 count the
consonants between the vowels in the ending and the first syllable before it

celestial   martial

confidential   substantial

essential   partial

impartial   potential

initial   presidential

residential	financial
sequential	commercial
torrential	official
beneficial	judicial
glacial	sacrificial

Worksheet 15 -ent| -ence |-ient |-ience

Count the consonants BETWEEN the vowel in the ending and the vowel in the first syllable back.
When there are 2 consonants the FIRST syllable back is stressed. When there are NO
Consonants or only ONE consonant the SECOND syllable back is stressed. See Rule #5 count the
consonants between the vowels in the ending and the first syllable before it

accent   coincident

accident   comment

agreement   competent

agreement   consent

apartment   compliment

element	conference
document	consequence
absence	consistence
circumference	existence
commence	excellence

convenient	ingredient
expedient	lenient
recipient	resilient
inconvenient	orient
nutrient	obedient

CHAPTER 10

STUDENT A – STUDENT B – STUDENT C

Student A Results

Beginning in February of the second semester of 3rd grade, 29 forty-minute, virtual lessons for phonemic training were begun. There were two in home visits completed. Student A's mother was present for all lessons, which helped to promote parent understanding of strategies used. Student A's mother also conducted 14 repeated reading practice sessions with the student in February, March, and April. Her mother is not a formally trained teacher.

Before Student A could work with CCVC or CVCC level syllables, this student needed to learn to discriminate between all the short vowel tones due to confusion with short /i/ and /e/, /e/ and /a/, /a/ and /u/ and /u/ and /o/. Student A had difficulty hearing the small changes between short vowel tones that were 'beside' each other in tongue and jaw placement when spoken. The mnemonic sentence "Is Eddy At Uncle Ollie's" was used to accomplish correct discrimination. The sentence "Long vowels sound like their letter name and short vowels go with the Eddy sentence." was used to help understand the difference between 'long' and 'short' vowel sounds.

In addition to vowel discrimination, Student A struggled to remember which direction to point the letters 'b' and 'd' when writing and which sound each made when decoding words. Student A was taught the strategy for feeling the sounds presented in Chapter 5 of this book. See the poster in Chapter 11.

After learning how to discriminate vowel tones and 'b' from 'd', Student A was able to proceed with voiced and voiceless consonant discrimination, /f/ /v/ and /th/ discrimination, etc.

Sessions followed the structure presented in Chapter 5 with the exception that we sometimes included two lists per session and devoted a few sessions to the phrasing strategy discussed in Chapter 8.

Multiple Syllable word reading, and writing was touched on in July during two sessions to refresh skills before returning to school in August. A few years have passed and Student A's mother reports that learning growth has continued. Student A still has an IEP with accommodations for extra time to complete tests and assignments but has not received further support from the SLP.

It is important to note that in 1st, 2nd and 3rd grades Student A received small group remedial reading instruction, intervention specialist instruction, and Orton Gillingham instruction. After 3- and one-half years [kindergarten, first, second and half of third grade] years in school, Student A managed to achieve reading fluency levels and comprehension scores that did not meet first grade standards of proficiency.

Whereas, after following the program in "20 Minute Phonemic Training for Dyslexia, Auditory Processing and Spelling" during the end of the second semester of 3rd grade , Student A's Reading and Spelling samples showed growth to 3rd grade level within a 4 month span of time.

Reading and Spelling Scores follow:

School Progress Report end of first semester grade 3: In June, the report card stated:

Reading beginning 3rd grade level text at 42 words per minute with 96% accuracy and 90% comprehension.

MAP reading scores:
Student A began the school year at 191 and was projected to finish at a 194.
Student A finished the school year at 204 exceeding fall projected score by 10 points. Student A read beginning 3rd grade level, Fountas and Pinnell Level N text, indicating an increase from level H to level N between December and May.

Classroom Writing Samples
Student A wrote two stories for the teacher in May.
Story 1 spelling accuracy 91%,
Story 2 spelling accuracy 96%
Word Level Spelling Sample
CVC score 87% accuracy
CCVC/CVCC 80% accuracy
Reading Out Loud Samples
School Fountas and Pinnell Level N, early 3rd Grade 42 Words Per Minute with 90% comprehension
Speech Language Pathologist reading sample:
81 words per minute with 96% accuracy using the same reading selection attempted in January Repeated reading selection with 3rd grade level text [Frye Readability Scale] 108 words per minute with greater than 95% accuracy.

Student B Results

Student B received in person lessons weekly in October and November of 2nd grade, after November circumstances for meeting changed due to family circumstances. We continued to meet virtually for an additional 28 sessions, on a sporadic basis, with poor internet connection, through February of 2nd grade.

After our first two months of actual 20-minute sessions [in 2nd grade], Student B made the following growth in reading and spelling skills: [16 sessions] which included the evaluation:

Student B's teacher reported reading a Fountas and Pinnell Level D when we began. Retesting from the classroom did not occur until a month later. No new data was available in November. Samples taken by SLP yielded:

Writing Sample: 83%   *[compared to 61.44% initially]*
Word Level Spelling Sample CVC 83% CCVC/CVCC 50% *[compared to 53% and 32% initially]*
Reading Fluency Sample: 2nd grade reading sample at 46 words per minute 89% accuracy *[in October read at 25 words per minute with 80% accuracy]*

One year later, in late October of 3rd grade, I was asked to take another look at Student B's progress. It should be noted that Student B was on an IEP by then. Strategies were shared with the Intervention Specialist working with Student B to provide added support for Student B.
On October 3rd grade Student B

read a first-grade level story [cold read] at 52 words per minute with 98% accuracy and a **2nd grade level story** at the same rate and level of accuracy.
after 3 repeated readings, increased rate to 104 words per minute on the 2nd grade level story. Student B's **writing sample** contained 85% spelling accuracy with only 3 phonemic errors in 34 words written.
 On the **word level tests** Student B spelled 70% of the CVC words correctly.

Sessions were conducted in Student B's classroom 3 to 4 times per month until early February. By then, Student B

read a 3rd grade level story at 73 words per minute with 100% accuracy
wrote 50 words in a writing sample with 82% accuracy.

Student C Results

Student C was seen for 9 thirty-minute sessions in the 3rd grade classroom between Halloween and Valentine's Day at the request of family due to concerns about Student 's spelling and writing skills.

School Progress Report end October grade 3:
1. Teacher reported that **Student C's reading was on grade level**, but writing contained many spelling errors causing writing products to be unreadable.
2. **Classroom Writing Samples**: first writing sample in October contained 51% correctly spelled words. After 9 sessions, in February, a writing sample for a prompt given by the SLP contained 82% correctly spelled words.
3. **Classroom writing samples for extended response questions** contained 73% correctly spelled words in early February.
4. **When given 9 dictated sentences** with 91 total words to write containing spelling patterns from the Word level assessments, Student C spelled 80% and 82% of the words correctly over two sessions.

Reading Out Loud Samples: On Halloween, Student C read a sample on 3rd grade level at 82 words per minute with 98% accuracy. No further reading samples were taken.

IN CONCLUSION

Schools are facing challenges never seen before. Proper implementation of strategies was difficult enough before 2020 and all the new obstacles posed today. As seen in the results between Students A, B and C, we can see the importance of the following when implementing any strategy for creating change:

1. must be appropriate to the condition for which it is designed.
2. must be applied. *[saying you will and actually executing the plan are miles apart!]*
3. must be applied correctly. *[not half-heartedly]*
4. must be applied with enough frequency. *[skipping lessons will work against your progress]*
5. must be applied with enough time in each lesson. *[giving it a couple of minutes and saying you did it will not work]*
6. must be applied over a long enough period as appropriate to the severity of the condition. *[it takes more than a week or two]*

I leave you with best wishes for success.

Student	Grade Level of Student Pre	Grade Level of Student Post	Reading at Grade Level Pre	Reading at Grade Level Post	Classroom Reading Rate Pre	Classroom Reading Rate Post	SLP Sample Reading Rate Pre	SLP Sample Reading Rate Post	Reading Accuracy Pre	Reading Accuracy Post	Reading Comprehension Fountas & Pinnell Pre	Reading Comprehension Fountas & Pinnell Post	Fountas & Pinnell Level Pre	Fountas & Pinnell Level Post	Authentic Writing Spelling Accuracy Pre	Authentic Writing Spelling Accuracy Post	Word Level Spelling Test Scores Pre CVC	Word Level Spelling Test Scores Pre CCVC/CVCC	Word Level Spelling Test Scores Post CVC	Word Level Spelling Test Scores Post CCVC/CVCC
A	Jan 3rd	May 3rd	below 1st	early 3rd	26 wpm 1st 38 wpm 2nd		1st GL 26 wpm 2nd GL 38 wpm 3rd GL text 39 wpm & 33 wpm		93% and 86%		70%		H & K		76% & 77%	91% 796%	76%	65%	87%	80%
B	Oct 2nd	March 2nd	preschool	NO DATA	NO DATA	NO DATA	Kdg Level 28 wpm 1st GL 57 wpm* 2nd GL 25 w pm	Kdg Level 73% 1st GL 93%* 2nd GL 80%	1st GL 52 2nd GL 52	1st & 2nd GL 98%	NO DATA	NO DATA	D	NO DATA	61.44%	83%	67%	40%	83%	50%
B was seen again 1 year later	Oct 3rd	Feb 3rd	2nd GL	3rd GL	NO DATA	NO DATA	1st & 2nd GL 46 wpm After repeated reading: 104 wpm	3rd GL 73 wpm	89%	100%	NO DATA	NO DATA	K	finished the school year at level N	85%	82%	70%	spelling was not addressed in these sessions since reading was the parent's primary concern.		
C	Oct 3rd	Feb 3rd	3rd GL	3rd GL	READING ON GRADE LEVEL										authentic: 51% & 73%	82%	no data could be taken since time was limited by services delivered in the classroom			

CHAPTER 11

SUPPLEMENTAL FORMS AND WORKSHEETS

SUGGESTED WRITING PROMPTS

- A Favorite Birthday

- Something they did recently

- Someplace they visited …. a vacation?

- How to…get ready for basketball practice

- How to…give your dog a bath

- How to play (name of favorite game)

- If I could fly, I would

- If I could turn back time, I would

- If I could be all grown up, I would

- We should wash our hands because…

- Retell a familiar story…3 Bears, 3 Little Pigs, Cinderella

- Retell a favorite movie they watched recently.

- Interview them. Ask them to write sentences to answer the questions.

- Where do you live?

- What was your favorite birthday and why?

- What was your favorite Christmas and why?

- What is the all-time favorite gift that you ever received? Why?

- What is your pet's name?

- What does your pet look like?

Word Level Assessment
List 1 CVC

1.	van	Mom drives a van.
2.	pit	A peach has a pit.
3.	mix	Stir up the cake mix.
4.	rob	He tried to rob the bank.
5.	chum	Your chum is your friend.
6.	mesh	A screen is made of wire mesh.
7.	chip	He ate one potato chip.
8.	shut	Please shut the door.
9.	thug	A thug is a bully.
10.	Beth	Her name is Beth.
11.	hide	Hide the present from her.
12.	rode	I rode my bike.
13.	gap	A path runs through the gap.
14.	wave	The wave washed the sand.
15.	gape	It is not polite to gape at people.
16.	sheet	Here is a clean sheet of paper.
17.	cot	He slept on a cot in the tent.
18.	feed	It is time to feed the dog.
19.	cut	Cut the paper in half.
20.	zit	A zit is a pimple.
21.	boss	She is the boss.
22.	fed	He fed the dog.
23.	sun	The sun went down.
24.	nip	The pony tried to nip me.
25.	buzz	Bees buzz.
26.	lid	Put a lid on the jar.
27.	bill	Pay the bill.
28.	mute	Mute the TV.
29.	wove	She wove a mat.
30.	cute	The cat is cute.

Assessment List 2 CCVC CVCC

1.   black   Black is a color.
2.   brake   My bike has a hand brake.
3.   flake   One flake of snow fell on my face.
4.   stack   Stack the books by the bed.
5.   track   Did you track in snow?
6.   brand   What brand of milk do you like?
7.   snake   I saw a snake on the road.
8.   strand   A strand of hair fell on the plate.
9.   drug   He drug his feet through the snow.
10. snug   Snug as a bug in a rug.
11. plot   A plot of corn grows by the road.
12. trick   The fox will trick the stork.
13. click   I heard a click.
14. spend   Spend some time at home.
15. plant   Plant the seeds in spring.
16. split   Split the clump of lilies.
17. spunk   The kitten has a lot of spunk.
18. blest   I am blest.
19. fret   Fret not, worry not; be happy.
20. crest   The river will crest today.
21. clunk   The motor went clunk and stopped.
22. drink   Drink all of your milk.
23. fling   Fling the petals around the floor.
24. glad   I am glad you are here.
25. print   Print your name.
26. grand   The grand party is over.
27. crack   There is a crack in the wall.
28. scold   Scold the dog for messing in the house.
29. Swung   He swung the bat and hit the ball.
30. slips   She slips on the ice a lot.
31. lists   The lists take a long time to write.
32. smoke   Smoke filled the room.
33. Husk   The corn has a husk on it.
34. frump   The frump did not comb her hair.
35. slump   Sit up so you do not slump.
36. glob   A glob of ink fell on the paper.
37. prize   He won the prize.
38. grape   The grape is green.
39. smack   Smack the ball hard.
40. Skunk   The skunk stinks.

Two Syllable Words – Doubling Consonants and -le syllables.

humble	He is a humble person.
pickle	I'll have dill pickle on my sandwich.
cuddle	The kitten will cuddle with me.
Brittle	The ice is brittle.
thimble	Use a thimble with a needle.
rattle	I hear a rattle in the engine.
dazzle	The magic show had a lot of dazzle.
bottle	Do you want a can or bottle?
fable	The "Fox and the Crow" is a fable.
bugle	Blow the bugle at dawn.
Bible	The Bible has 66 books.
table	lay it on the table.
maple	the maple tree has leaves.
candle	Blow out the candle.
handle	The handle is hot.
rustle	The leaves rustle in the wind.
raffle	He won the raffle.
cripple	The trap can cripple an animal.
settle	Will you settle for ice cream?
jungle	The jungle is full of monkeys.
cradle	The cradle is for the new baby.
bridle	Put the bridle on the horse.
staple	You can staple the papers together.
ruffle	The bird's feathers ruffle in the wind.
buckle	Buckle up your seat belt.
drizzle	It will drizzle rain all day!

Word List 1 Grid of Sounds Sample

	p b m w	t d n s z	r l	f v th	k g h x	sh ch j	short vowel	long vowel	ck	final e
van		n		v			a			
pit	p	t					i			
mix	m				x		i			
rob	b		r				o			
chum	m					ch	u			
mesh	m					xsh	e			
chip	p					ch	i			
shut		t				sh	u			
thug				th	g		u			
beth	b			th			e			
hide		d			h			i		ide
rode		d	r					o		ode
gap	p				g		a			
wave	w			v				o		ove
gape	p				g			a		ape
sheet		t				sh		e		eet
cot		t			K[c]		o			
feed		d		f				e		eed
cut		t			K [c]		x			

	p b m w	t d n S	r l	f v th	k g h	sh ch j	Short vowel	long vowel	floss	Final e
zit		z t					i			
boss	b	s					o		ss	
fed		d		f			e			
sun		s n					u			
nip	p	n					i			
buzz	b	z					u		zz	
lid		d	l				i			
bill	b		l				i		ll	
mute	m	t					u			te
wove	w			v				o		ve
cute		t			K [c]			u		te

Word List 2 Grid of Sounds Sample

	p b m w	t d n s z	r l	f v th	k g h	sh ch j	Short vowel	long vowel	-ck	final e
black	bl		bl	.	k		a		ck	
brake	br		br					a		ke
flake			fl	fl	k			a		ke
stack		st			k		a		ck	
track		tr	r		k		a		ck	
brand	br	nd	br				a			
snake		sn			k			a		ke
strand		str nd	str				a			
drug		dr	rd		g		u			
snug		sn			g		u			
plot	pl	t	pl				o			
trick		tr	tr		k		i		ck	
click			cl		Cl k		i		ck	
spend	sp	sp nd					e			
plant	pl	nt	l				a			
split	spl	spl t	spl				i			
spunk	sp	sp nk			nk		u			
blest	bl	st					e			
fret		t	fr	fr			e			
crest		st	r		cr		e			

	p b m w	t d n s z	r l	f v th	k g h ng	sh ch j	Short vowel	long vowel	-ck	final e
clunk		nk	cl		cl nk		u			
drink		dr nk	dr		nk		i			
fling			fl	fl	ng		i			
glad		gl d			gl		a			
print	pr	nt	pr				i			
grand		nd	gr		gr		a			
crack			cr		cr		a		k	
scold		Sc ld	ld					o		
swung	sw	sw			ng		u			
slips	ps	Sl ps					i			
lists		sts	l				i			
smoke		sm			k		o			ke
husks		sks			h sks		u			
frump	mp		fr				u			
slump	mp	sl	sl				u			
glob	b		gl		gl		o			
prize	pr	z						i		ze
grape	p		gr		gr			a		
smack	sm	sm			k		a		ck	
skunk		Sk nk			nk		u			

TYPES OF SPELLING ERRORS REFERENCE [Reading or Writing]

Phonemic: [PHE} Errors related to the sounds. Sounds left out [omission]*["split" spelled or pronounced "pit"]* , added [insertion] *["brake" pronounced or spelled ; "burake,"* a different sound used than the letter seen, or different letter written than the sound in the word *[look pronounced or written as "wut,"* sounds switched around in the order they are in a word, *["crab" spoken or written as "carb."*

Phonic: [PHO] either misapplying or not observing phonic rules for letter patterns *["lik" for "lick" | "fech" for" fetch" etc.] See Chapter 8 for more details.*

Semantic: [SEM] mixing up words that sound the same but are spelled differently. *[to, too, two o   r there, their, they're].*

Mental Orthographic Imagery: [MOI] and **Sight Words** Misspelling or pronouncing words that do not follow normal rules for phonics or sound to letter relationships. *["**know**" pronounced as "now" or spelled as "'no" | "lamb" spelled as "lam" | "when" spelled as "w"']*

TYPES OF PHONEMIC [SOUND] ERRORS REFERENCE

Vowel Discrimination: Writing or reading short vowels /i/ for /e/, /u/ for /a/, /e/ for /a/, /u/ for /o/, /o/ for /u/ or confusing long and short vowel spellings by adding the final e for short vowels but not for long vowels.

Sequencing sounds correctly: Reversing the order of sounds in words when reading or the letter order for the sounds when spelling. Writing or reading *"tried" for "turned" or "straight" as "strat" or "start."*

Omissions: Leaving sounds out of words when reading or writing such as *"back" for "black"*

Insertions: Adding extra sounds to words when reading or writing such as reading *"string" for "sting"* or *"sing"* or adding a sound between letters in blends *"burake" for "break."*

Substitutions: using the wrong letter when writing or sound when reading. *"fing" for "'thing" | "'tat'" for "cat" |"bwue" for "blue"*

When a child has an articulation impairment and is not able to speak some sounds, this must be considered when they are reading. Do not count their articulation errors as reading errors. However, if they spell words using the wrong letters for the sounds, count the mistakes as spelling errors.

Name of student	JOE					Name of Sample		MY DOG		
Date of Sample	JAN 20 2016	# words written	18	# words correct	26	Subtract number of misspelled words from Total Words Written to ge number of words spelled correctly. Divide number of words spelled correctly by number of words written. [Ex: 18-4 IS 14. 14 DIVIDED BY 18 IS 78%]				78%

PHE IS PHONEMIC ERROR   PHO IS PHONIC ERROR   SEM IS SEMANTIC ERROR   MOI IS MENTAL ORTHOGRAPHIC IMAGE ERROR
DNA MEANS 'DOES NOT APPLY'

Word Missed	Student Spelling	PHE	PHO	SEM	MOI
string	tin	n for ng; s and r	DNA	DNA	DNA
our	are	DNA	DNA	are for our	DNA
when	wen				wen for when
stick	stik	DNA	k for ck	DNA	DNA
					TOTAL ALL
	TOTALS ->	1	1	1	1	4
	PERCENT	25%	25%	25.00%	25%	
	divide number in each column					
	by total of all errors					

Name of student				Name of Sample				
Date of Sample		# words written	# words correct	Subtract number of misspelled words from Total Words Written to ge number of words spelled correctly. Divide number of words spelled correctly by number of words written. [Ex: 18-4 IS 14. 14 DIVIDED BY 18 IS 78%]				%

PHE IS PHONEMIC ERROR   PHO IS PHONIC ERROR   SEM IS SEMANTIC ERROR   MOI IS MENTAL ORTHOGRAPHIC IMAGE ERROR

DNA MEANS 'DOES NOT APPLY'

Word Missed	Student Spelling	PHE		PHO		SEM		MOI
									TOTAL ALL
	TOTALS ->							
	PERCENT	%		%		%		%
	divide number in each column							
	by total of all errors							

KINDS OF SOUND ERRORS SORTING SAMPLE CHART

Name of student Joe						
Date of Sample	Mar-18	Name of Sample : My Kite				
Word Missed	**Student Spelling**	**VOWEL**	**OMITTED SOUND**	**INSERTED SOUND**	**REVERSED**	**SUBSTITUTED**
cut	cot	o/u				
black	bak		L			
broke	burok	o/oke		bur/br		
turn	trun				ru/ur	
kite	tet	e/I i/ite				t/k
						Total All
	TOTALS ->	3	1	1	1	1	7
	PERCENT	43%	14%	14%	14%	14%	100%

To gind percentage for each column: divide number in each TOTALS column by TOTAL number of phonemic errors

KINDS OF ERRORS SORTING CHART

Name of student						
Date of Sample		Name of Sample :				

Word Missed	Student Spelling	VOWEL	OMITTED SOUND	INSERTED SOUND	REVERSED	SUBSTITUTED	
							Total All
	TOTALS ->						
	PERCENT	%	%	%	%	%	%

To find percentage for each column: divide number in each TOTALS column by TOTAL number of phonemic errors

SOUND PLAY SAMPLES
USE THIS FORM TO WRITE WHAT YOUR CHILD TELLS YOU WHEN YOU ASK THEM TO:

- A. Blend sounds to make a word. Example you say /k/ + /a/+/t/   They answer 'cat'
- B. Tell you every sound in a word.   Example: you say 'cat'   They say /k/ /a/ /t/.
    1. You say 'black'   They say /b/ /u/ /l/ /a/ /k/
    2. This is a mistake. You want to know this. Write exactly what they said.
- C. Take sounds away to make a new word. Example You say 'cat' Take away the first sound.
    - i. They say 'at'
    - ii. You say 'meet' take away the last sound.   They say 'me'
- D. Add sounds to make a new word. Example: You say 'cat' add a /s/ to the beginning. What is the word?
    - i. They say 'scat'
- E. Change a sound to make a new word. Example: You say 'cat' change the middle sound to /u/.
    - i. They say 'cut'

You have more than 10 words in each test. Choose those that you feel would be best for you and your student. Try to have them do 10 words for each test. If they miss 4 out of the first 5 they try, STOP. Mark that section "not testable." Write down exactly what the student says for each word missed.

A. Blending

1)_____   2)_____   3)_____   4)_____

5)_____   5)_____   7)_____   8)_____

9)_____   10)_____   11)_____   12)_____

13)_____   14)_____   15)_____   16)_____

B Segmenting

1)_____   2)_____   3)_____   4)_____

5)_____   5)_____   7)_____   8)_____

10)_____   10)_____   11)_____   12)_____

12)_____   14)_____   15)_____   16)_____

C. Deleting

1)_____   2)_____   3)_____   4)_____

5)_____   6)_____   7)_____   8)_____

9)_____   10)_____   11)_____   12)_____

13)_____   14)_____   15)_____   16)_____

C Deleting   2)_____   3)_____   4)_____

1)_____   6)_____   7)_____   8)_____

5)_____   10)_____   11)_____   12)_____

9)_____   14)_____   15)_____   16)_____

13)_____

D Inserting   2)_____   3)_____   4)_____

1)_____   6)_____   7)_____   8)_____

5)_____   10)_____   11)_____   12)_____

9)_____   14)_____   15)_____   16)_____

13)_____

E. Substituting   2)_____   3)_____   4)_____

1)_____   6)_____   7)_____   8)_____

5)_____   10)_____   11)_____   12)_____

9)_____   14_____   15)_____   16)_____

13)_____

1. Blending Say each sound [phoneme] separate from all the others.
    Be sure that you do not add an extra sound after a phoneme.
    Be sure to put a space between each sound.

1) p -a -t   2) c-a-ne   3) s-n-i-p   4) l-a-m-p

5) sh-i-n   6) p-i- le   7) s-m-e-ll   8) s-e-n-d

9) f-e-ll   10) s-ea-l   11) s-t-a-ck   12) r-i-n-k

13) m-o-ck 14) m-u-l-e   15) t-r-u-dge   16) l-a-s-t

17) n-u-dge 18) v-o-te   19) f-l -o-ck   20) l-i-f-t

2. Segmenting. This time you will say the word and your student will separate
the phonemes. Be sure to make a note if they add a sound to the end of a phoneme.

1) sat   2) tame   3) snail   4) jump

1) pin   6) file   7) smack   8) lend

9) fall   10) peel   11) stem   12) rust

13) sock   14) cool   15) fruit   16) list

3. Deleting sounds at the beginning and end of a word.

Example: You ask them to say 'cat' and then say it without the /k/ sound. What is the new word?

1) sat [no /s/]   2) tame [no /t/]   3) grade [no /g/]   4) cold [no /d/]

5) pin [no /p/]   6) file [no /f/]   7) trust [no /t/]   8) herd [no /d/]

9) fall [no /f/]   10) peel [no /p/]   11) spoke [no /s/]   12) growth /no /th/]

13) chair [no /ch/]   14) shade [no /sh/   15) bridge [no /b/]   16) style [no /l/]

Deleting sounds in the middle and end of words.

1) shelf [no /f/]   2) note [no /t/]   3) sneak [no /n/]   4) send [no /n/]

5) goat [no /t/]   6) soak [no /k/]   7) truck [no /r/]   8) list [no /s/]

9) ride [no /d/]   10) tire [no /r/]   11) smoke [no /m/]   12) lent [no /n/]

13) pace [no /s/]   14) wrench [no /ch/]   15) stand [no /t/]   16) lent [no /n/]

17) sail [no /l/]   18) tooth [no /th/]   19) slack [no /l/]   20) belt [no /l/]

ANSWERS

1) shell   2) not   3) seek   4) said

5) go   6) so   7) tuck   8) lit

9) rye   10) tie   11) soak   12) let

13) pay   14) wren   15) sand   16) let

17) say   18) too   19) sack   20 bet

4. Inserting sounds at the beginning, middle and end.
   Example: Say 'cat'. Now ask your student to say it again but add /s/ to the beginning. What is the word now?

1) [/s/] not	2) [/r/] oat	3) [/l/] seep	4) [/d/] men
5) [/r/] at	6) [/v/] oat	7) [/r/] keep	8) [/t/] mis
9) [/b/] it	10) [/g/] on	11) [/m/]soak	12) [/t/] fell
13) [/f/] add	14) [/l/] it	15) [/n/] sip	16) [/f/] sell

ANSWERS

1) snot	2) wrote	3) sleep	4) mend
5) rat	6) vote	7) creep	8) mist
9) bit	10) gone	11) smoke	12) felt
13) fad	14) lit	15) snip	16) self

5. Substituting sounds at the beginning and in the middle of words. Example: Say cat. Now ask your student to say it again but take out the /k/ and put in an /f/ sound. What is the word now? [fat] Say 'cloak'. Now say it again but take out the second sound /l/, and make it an /r/, [croak]. It is okay to use the flat marbles or colored pieces of paper as you show your student what to do. Allow them to use these tools when answering.

1) [/g/] not	2) [/r/] vice	3) [/s/] flap	4) /l/ crown
5) [/i/ at	6) [/k/ reap	7) [/g/] brand	8) /t/ slop
9) [a] it	10) [/b/] phone	11) [/b/] fend	12) /m/ stoke
13) [/b/] fit	14) [/f/] fail	15) [/d/] health	16) /s/ rent

ANSWERS

1) Got	2) rice	3) slap	4) clown
5) it	6) keep	7) grand	8) stop
9) at	10) bone	11) bend	12) smoke
13) bit	14) tail	15) held	16) rest

Reading Fluency Calculation Formula
Calculating Words Per Minute and Accuracy

Write the amount of time your student read at the end of their reading.

If you stopped before the end of the story, mark the place where they stopped reading.

Write down how many words they read.

Count the number of words missed. Subtract that number from the number of total words

the child read. Divide the number of words missed by the number of words read.

Example: 68 words read. 7 words were missed.

68 words -7 mistakes = 61 words read correctly

61   words read correctly

------   = 89%   89% accuracy

68 total words read

Next calculate the number of words per minute they read.

Turn the minutes and seconds into all seconds. For example, if they read

For 2 minutes and 40 seconds, you would multiply 60 seconds x 2 minutes = 120 seconds

120 seconds + 40 seconds = 160 seconds. Next you will divide the number of words they

Read [in our example it was 68 words] by 160 seconds and multiply THAT answer by 60.

Example: (60 seconds x 2 minutes) + 40 seconds = 160 seconds reading

68 words read

____ = .425 x 60 seconds = 25.5 words per minute

160 number of seconds reading

So, we know our student read 25.5 words per minute with 89% accuracy.

SUMMARY PAGE

Name:	Date:	Date:	Date:
Authentic Writing			
Word List 1			
Word List 2			
Word List 3			
Blending CVC			
Blending CCVC-CVCC			
Segmenting CVC			
Segmenting CCVC-CVCC			
Deleting CVC			
Deleting CCVC-CVCC			
Inserting CVC			
Inserting CCVC-CVCC			
Substituting CVC			
Substituting CCVC-CVCC			
Reverse CVC			
Reverse CVC-CVCC			
Discriminating between voiced & voiceless sounds			
Discriminating between short vowel tones			
Reading Selection Level			
Reading Accuracy			
Reading Rate--Words Per Minute			
Reading Selection Level			
Reading Accuracy			
Reading Rate--Words Per Minute			
Reading Selection Level			
Reading Accuracy			
Reading Rate--Words Per Minute			
Reading errors deletions:			
Reading errors inserting:			
Reading errors substituting:			
Sound and letter errors PRE:			
Sound and letter errors POST:			
PHONIC RULES PRE:			

Front Vowels Lip and Mouth Photos

FRONT VOWELS

ee *feed*

I *it*

e *Eddy*

ae *ate*

a *at*

u *uncle*

o *Ollie*

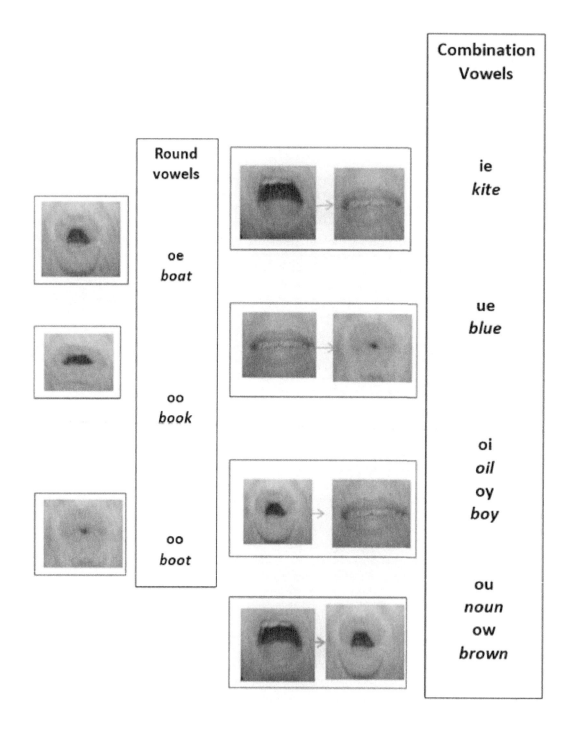

Round vowels

oe
boat

oo
book

oo
boot

Combination Vowels

ie
kite

ue
blue

oi
oil
oy
boy

ou
noun
ow
brown

Vowel Face

Lip, Jaw and Tongue Placement
for Vowel Sounds

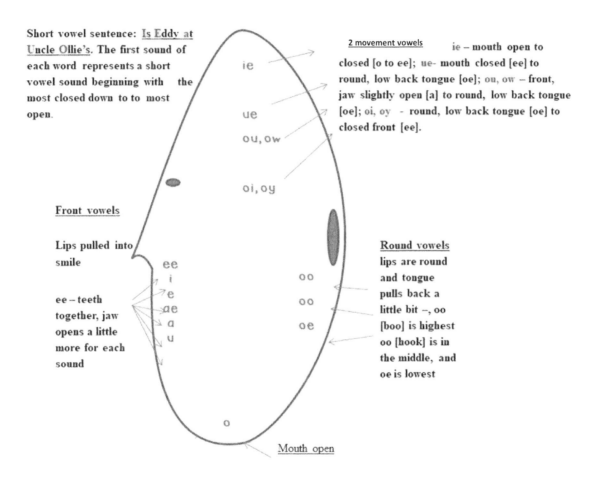

Short vowel sentence: Is Eddy at Uncle Ollie's. The first sound of each word represents a short vowel sound beginning with the most closed down to to most open.

2 movement vowels   ie – mouth open to closed [o to ee]; ue- mouth closed [ee] to round, low back tongue [oe]; ou, ow – front, jaw slightly open [a] to round, low back tongue [oe]; oi, oy - round, low back tongue [oe] to closed front [ee].

ie

ue

ou, ow

oi, oy

Front vowels

Lips pulled into smile

ee – teeth together, jaw opens a little more for each sound

ee
i
e
ae
a
u

oo

oo

oe

Round vowels
lips are round and tongue pulls back a little bit –, oo [boo] is highest oo [hook] is in the middle, and oe is lowest

o

Mouth open

Part 1 PHONIC RULE POSTER

SHORT VOWEL PHONIC RULES

Sound for the Letter Name is turned
OFF

1. There is NO /e/ on the end of the syllable.

can, ten, kit, not, cut

2. FLOSS When the last sound is /f/ /l/ or /s/, there will usually be two of 's', 'l', or 'f' letters.

The word FLOSS is a mnemonic to help them remember this. It contains all three sounds, has a short vowel and two 's' letters on the end.

hill, fell, cuff, mess, stuff, boss

Common exceptions: bus, gas, us, yes

3. When the last sound in a one syllable word is /k/, it is spelled ck.

tack, check, lick, smock, duck

LONG VOWEL PHONIC RULES

Sound for the Letter Name is turned
ON

1. An /e/ on the end of the syllable is one of three ways to make a vowel turn 'on.'

cane, teen, note, cute Note: long /e/ letters often stay together
weed, seed, feed,

2. When a vowel is long, you do not add two /l/ /f/ or /s/ letters at the end, just add the final /e/.

lake, pile, fuse, feel, pose race*

[*note that sometimes –ce is used to maintain the /s/ sound from becoming a /z/ sound when pronounced]

3. When the final sound is /k/ just add an /e/ to the end. DO NOT USE –ck.

Take, cheek, like, smoke, duke

SHORT VOWEL PHONIC RULES

Sound for the Letter Name is turned
OFF

4.   When /ch/ is on the end of a one syllable word, it is usually spelled –tch or -nch.

match, butch, pitch, punch, pinch
Common exceptions include:
Rich, much, such, which, touch

5.   When the final sound in a one syllable word is /j/, it will be spelled –dge.

fudge, hedge, ridge, badge, dodge

6. When a one syllable or two-syllable word has a short vowel and: *you are adding an ending beginning with a vowel

[–ing, -ed, -est, -er or -y,]
AND there is only one consonant after the vowel THEN: double the last consonant to keep the first syllable closed and the vowel short.

hop / hopping   big / biggest
fun / funny
mop / mopped   rub / rubber
fill / filled

LONG VOWEL PHONIC RULES

Sound for the Letter Name is turned
ON

4.   A double letter vowel spelling is used for the long vowel before the /ch/.

Each, reach, coach

5. When the final sound in a one syllable word is /j/, it is spelled –ge. /J/ is never used as the last letter in an English word.

Huge, change, page, gage

6.   When a one syllable word has a long vowel, drop the /e/ and add -ing, -ed, -est, -or, –er.
facing, faced, racer, posing, piling, piled, wisest, hoping, hoped, taped, taping

When a two syllable word has a long vowel in the first syllable, there will only be one consonant between the vowel in the first and second syllables. This allows the first syllable to be an open syllable and is the second way a long vowel sound is created in a syllable.
ma ple ba by di ner su per.

SHORT VOWEL PHONIC RULES
Sound for the Letter Name is turned
OFF

LONG VOWEL PHONIC RULES
Sound for the Letter Name is turned
ON

7. When a two-syllable word ends with a short vowel and one consonant, double the final consonant as in number 6.

ruf fle/ *ruf fled / ruf fling*

7. When the second syllable in a two-syllable word has a long vowel sound, do not double the final consonant.

Admire / admiring / admired

8. When spelling a two-syllable word and the first syllable has a short vowel, there is usually a consonant at the end of the first syllable & one at the beginning of the second syllable making the first syllable closed.

lit tle | hap pen | sud den | lic king sup per | din ner} mus tard

8. When spelling a two- syllable word and the first syllable has a long vowel, there will not be a consonant at the end of the first syllable. The syllable is open which makes it sound long.

li king, su per, ru dest, fi nal, re sist

Short Vowel Phonic Rules

Sound for the Letter Name is Turned

OFF

1. **There is NO /e/ on the end of the word.**
   can, ten, kit, not, cut

Long Vowel Phonic Rules

Sound for the Letter Name is Turned

ON

1. **An /e/ on the end of the word is one of three ways to make a vowel turn 'on.'**

   cane, teen, note, cute

(Note: long vowel /e/ is usually 'ee' in the middle of the word)

Short Vowel Phonic Rules

Sound for the Letter Name is turned

OFF

2. **FLOSS When the last sound is /f/ /l/ or /s/,**

there will usually be two of them.

The word FLOSS is a mnemonic to help them remember this. It contains all three sounds, has a short vowel and two 's' letters on the end.

Long Vowel Phonic Rules

Sound for the Letter Name is turned

ON

2. When a vowel is long, you do not add two /l/ /f/ or /s/ letters at the end, just add the final /e/.
pile, fuse, feel, pose, race

[*note that –ce is used to maintain the /s/ sound from becoming a /z/ sound when pronounced]

Short Vowel Phonic Rules

Sound for the Letter Name is turned

OFF

3. When the last sound in a one syllable word is /k/, it is spelled –ck.

tack, check, lick, smock, duck

Long Vowel Phonic Rules

Sound for the Letter Name is turned

ON

3. When the final sound is /k/ just add an /e/ to the end. DO NOT USE –ck.

Take, cheek, like, smoke, duke

Short Vowel Phonic Rules

Sound for the Letter Name is turned

OFF

4. When /ch/ is on the end of a one syllable word, it is usually spelled –tch or -nch.

match, butch, pitch, punch, pinch
Common exceptions include:
rich much, such, which

Long Vowel Phonic Rules

Sound for the Letter Name is turned

ON

4. A double letter vowel spelling is used for the long vowel before the /ch/.
Each, reach, coach

Short Vowel Phonic Rules

Sound for the Letter Name is turned

OFF

5. When the final sound in a one syllable

word is /j/, it will be spelled –dge.

fudge, hedge, ridge, badge, dodge

Long Vowel Phonic Rules

Sound for the Letter Name is turned

ON

5. When the final sound in a one syllable word is /j/, it is spelled –ge.   /j/ is never used as the last letter in an English word.

Huge, change, page, gage

Short Vowel Phonic Rules
Sound for the Letter Name is turned
OFF

6. When a one syllable or two-syllable word has a short vowel and: *you are adding an ending beginning with a vowel

[–ing, -ed, -est, -er or -y,]

AND there is only one consonant after the vowel
THEN: double the last consonant to keep the first syllable closed and the vowel short.

hop / hopping   big / biggest   fun / funny
mop / mopped   rub / rubber   fill / filled

Long Vowel Phonic Rules
Sound for the Letter Name is turned
ON

6. When a one syllable word has a long vowel, drop the /e/ and add -ing, -ed, -est, -or –er.

facing, faced, racer, posing, piling, piled, wisest, hoping, hoped, taped, taping,

When a two syllable word has a long vowel in the first syllable, there will only be one consonant between the vowel in the first and second syllables. This allows the first syllable to be an open syllable and is the second way a long vowel sound is created in a syllable .

Short Vowel Phonic Rules
Sound for the Letter Name is turned OFF

7. When a two-syllable word ends with a short vowel and one consonant, double the final consonant as in number 6.
ruf fle/ *ruf fled / ruf fling*

Long Vowel Phonic Rules
Sound for the Letter Name is turned ON

7. When the second syllable in a two syllable word and has a long vowel sound, do not double the final consonant.
Admire / admiring / admired

Short Vowel Phonic Rules
Sound for the Letter Name is turned
OFF
8 . When you spell a two syllable word and the first
syllable has a short vowel,
there is usually a consonant at the end of the first
syllable & one at the beginning of the second syllable.
[the first syllable is closed]
lit tle | hap pen | sud den | lic king |sup per din
ner | mus tard

Long Vowel Phonic Rules
Sound for the Letter Name is turned
ON
8. When you spell a two syllable word and the first
syllable has a long vowel, there will not be a
consonant at the end of the first syllable to keep the
syllable open and make the vowel long.
Li king | su per | ru dest | fi nal| re sist

STUDENT WORK
PAGE CCVC

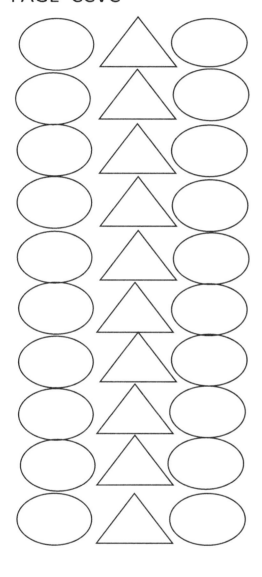

WRITING PRACTICE

1._____

2._____

3._____

4._____

5._____

6._____

7._____

8._____

9._____

10._____

Student Name: _____Date _____ Page Number_____ List Number_____

Blending _____/ 10   Segmenting _____/10   Tracking Changes _____/10   Reading _____/10

Spelling _____/10   Sentence Writing % _____ Phonic Rules presented: FLOSS ck tch dge Doubling

CCV Student Worksheet

STUDENT WORK
PAGE CCV

WRITING PRACTICE

1._____

2._____

3._____

4._____

5._____

6._____

7._____

8._____

9._____

10._____

Student Name: _____Date _____ Page Number_____ List Number_____

Blending _____/ 10   Segmenting _____/10   Tracking Changes _____/10   Reading _____/10

Spelling _____/10   Sentence Writing % _____ Phonic Rules presented: FLOSS ck tch   dge Doubling

STUDENT WORK
PAGE CCVC

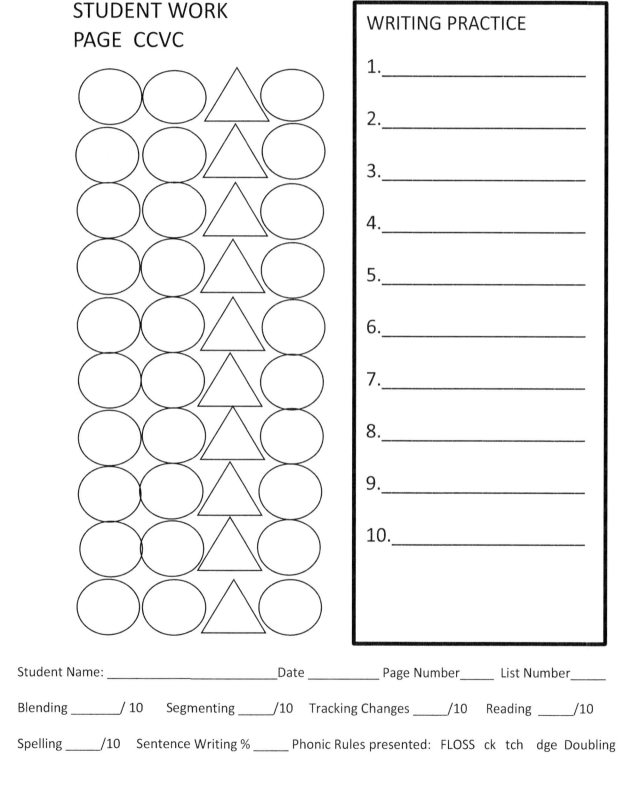

WRITING PRACTICE

1._____

2._____

3._____

4._____

5._____

6._____

7._____

8._____

9._____

10._____

Student Name: _____Date _____ Page Number_____ List Number_____

Blending _____/ 10   Segmenting _____/10   Tracking Changes _____/10   Reading _____/10

Spelling _____/10   Sentence Writing % _____ Phonic Rules presented: FLOSS ck tch   dge Doubling

CVCC Student Worksheet

STUDENT WORK
PAGE CVCC

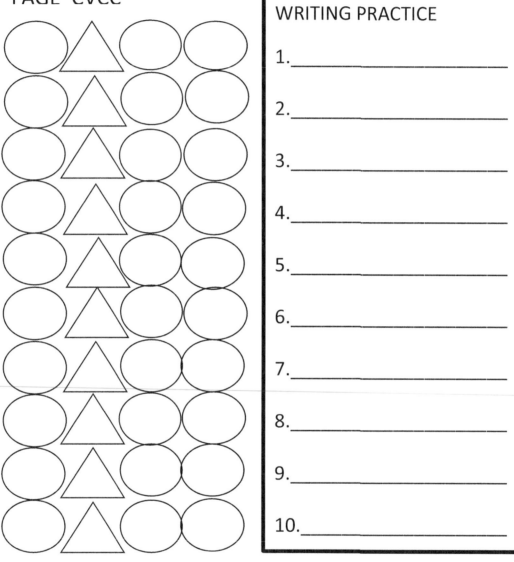

WRITING PRACTICE

1._____

2._____

3._____

4._____

5._____

6._____

7._____

8._____

9._____

10._____

Student Name: _____Date _____ Page Number_____ List Number_____

Blending _____/ 10   Segmenting _____/10   Tracking Changes _____/10   Reading _____/10

Spelling _____/10   Sentence Writing % _____ Phonic Rules presented: FLOSS ck tch dge Doubling

STUDENT WORK
PAGE CCVCC

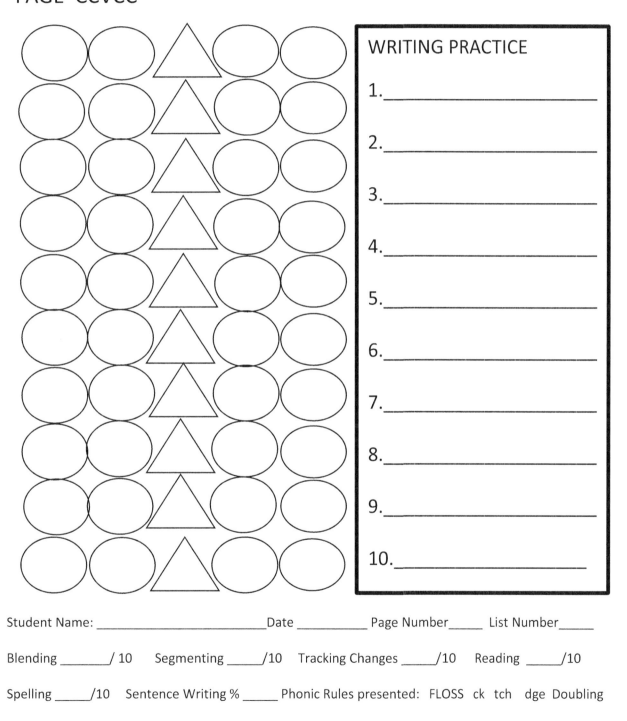

WRITING PRACTICE

1._____

2._____

3._____

4._____

5._____

6._____

7._____

8._____

9._____

10._____

Student Name: _____Date _____ Page Number_____ List Number_____

Blending _____/ 10   Segmenting _____/10   Tracking Changes _____/10   Reading _____/10

Spelling _____/10   Sentence Writing % _____ Phonic Rules presented: FLOSS ck tch   dge Doubling

Lesson Recording Sheet

Observational Notes for 20 Minute Phonemic Lesson

_____

_____

_____

_____

_____

_____

Name _____Date _____Page:_____List _____

Sound Target_____ Phonic Rule Target_____

Blend _____/10   Sound Change Tracking _____/10

Segmenting _____/10   Deleting_____/_____Inserting _____/_____

Reading: _____/10 Words Spelling _____/10 Words

Writing Sentences_____/_____Words ____%

Repeated Reading : Best of 3 WPM _____Accuracy%_____ Reading Level_____

Story Title:_____ Cold Read Y/N

Line/Paragraph # read_____

Leveled Reading Passage 1

Story 1: Bill and Tom Go Fishing	Early to Mid 1st grade		
		Words Per	
	Line	Paragraph	Total
Bill and Tom live next door to each other. Bill has a big cat and a small dog.	18	18	18
Tom has a small cat and a big dog. Bill and Tom both like to fish. Tom cannot	18	36	36
fish alone. Bill cannot fish alone. But they can go fish with each	13	49	49
other. They like to fish off the bank of the lake near town. They both can	16	65	65
walk the six blocks to get there. They carry their poles and bait. The dogs	15	80	80
like to go too. The cats cannot come. They want to eat the fish!	14	94	94
One day they went when they first woke up. A lot of fish were by the	16	16	110
end of the pier. It was like the fish wanted them to catch them! Bill	15	31	125
put his line in the water first. His line went down. It had a big catfish on it.	18	49	143
Then Tom put his line in the water. His line went down too. It had a big	17	66	160
trout on it. They wanted to eat trout. Bill tried again. This time his line	15	81	175
did have a trout on it.	6	87	181
Bill said, "Let's give the cats a treat. Let's give them the catfish and we can	16	16	197
eat the trout." The two boys took the fish home. They cut the scales off and	16	32	213
took out the bones. Their moms said they would fry the fish for them.	14	46	227
They ate a big meal of fried trout. The cats shared a big meal of catfish.	17	63	244
The dogs did not get any fish, but they did get to play in the park by the lake.	19	82	263

Story 1: Bill and Tom Go Fishing

Bill and Tom live next door to each other. Bill has a big cat and a small dog. Tom has a small cat and a big dog. Bill and Tom both like to fish. Tom cannot fish alone. Bill cannot fish alone. But they can go fish with each other. They like to fish off the bank of the lake near town. They both can walk the six blocks to get there. They carry their poles and bait. The dogs like to go too. The cats cannot come. They want to eat the fish!

One day they went when they first woke up. A lot of fish were by the end of the pier. It was like the fish wanted them to catch them! Bill put his line in the water first. His line went down. It had a big catfish on it. Then Tom put his line in the water. His line went down too. It had a big trout on it. They wanted to eat trout. Bill tried again. This time his line did have a trout on it.

Bill said, "Let's give the cats a treat. Let's give them the catfish and we can eat the trout." The two boys took the fish home. They cut the scales off and took out the bones. Their moms said they would fry the fish for them. They ate a big meal of fried trout. The cats shared a big meal of catfish. The dogs did not get any fish, but they did get to play in the park by the lake.

Leveled Reading Passage 2

Story 2:   The Pet Race

	Words Per	
Line	Paragraph	Total

Bill and Tom like to run. When they race, Bill wins some and Tom	14	14	14
wins some. But the dogs win each time! Bill's small dog's name is Pete.	14	28	28
Tom's big dog's name is Shep. It would seem that Shep should run faster	14	42	42
than Pete. That is not the case. Pete runs faster than Shep or Bill or	15	57	57
Tom!	1	58	58
Bill and Tom's town have a pet race in June each year. They wanted	14	14	72
to see if Pete or Shep could win the race. So, they started running with	15	29	87
the dogs every day. They ran in many places. They ran to the park.	14	43	101
They ran around the lake. They ran to the Shell gas station to get	14	57	115
things for their mom. They ran to the car wash to see the boys cleaning	15	72	130
cars. Each time they ran Pete and Shep ran too. They did this all through	15	87	145
April and May.	3	90	148
When it was time for the race, they ran the same path that the race	15	15	163
would follow. Pete and Shep seemed to like to run with Bill and Tom.	14	29	177
But Bill and Tom did not know if the dogs would run as well without	15	44	192
Bill and Tom. What could they do to make sure the dogs would run?	14	58	206
Bill had an idea. He told Tom to go to the start and Bill would wait	16	74	222
at the end of the path. Bill had a big bone for a prize at the end. Tom	18	92	240
held the dogs. He counted three and let them go when Bill picked up	14	106	254
the bones. Both dogs ran. They wanted those bones! It worked. Bill	12	118	266
and Tom, Shep and Pete were all ready to race.	10	128	276
On race day Bill got a big bone with meat on it for Shep and a small	17	17	293
bone with meat on it for Pete. The boys had to think of one more thing.	16	33	309
How would they show the bone to the dogs with all the other pets,	15	48	324
boys and girls there? They put the bones in bags. When the race started,	14	62	338
Bill and Tom stood by the end line and took the bones out of the bags.	16	78	354
ALL the dogs saw the bones and ran to Bill and Tom! Shep and Pete	15	93	369
ran like the wind. Both dogs got there first. They got the bones and	14	107	383
Shep won the race. Pete was not the fastest dog today.	11	118	394
The other kids had treats for their dogs too, but did not like that Bill	15	15	409
and Tom's dogs won. They made a rule that no kid could show a treat	15	30	424
when the dogs ran the race. Kids had to give the dogs a treat when the	16	46	440
race was over.	3	49	443

Story 2: The Pet Race

Bill and Tom like to run. When they race, Bill wins some and Tom wins some. But the dogs win each time! Bill's small dog's name is Pete. Tom's big dog's name is Shep. It would seem that Shep should run faster than Pete. That is not the case. Pete runs faster than Shep or Bill or Tom!

Bill and Tom's town have a pet race in June each year. They wanted to see if Pete or Shep could win the race. So, they started running with the dog's every day. They ran in many places. They ran to the park. They ran around the lake. They ran to the Shell gas station to get things for their mom. They ran to the car wash to see the boys cleaning cars. Each time they ran, Pete and Shep ran too. They did this all through April and May.

When it was time for the race, they ran the same path that the race would follow. Pete and Shep seemed to like to run with Bill and Tom. But Bill and Tom did not know if the dogs would run as well without Bill and Tom. What could they do to make sure the dogs would run?

Bill had an idea. He told Tom to go to the start and Bill would wait at the end of the path. Bill had a big bone for a prize at the end. Tom held the dogs. He counted three and let them go when Bill picked up the bones. Both dogs ran. They wanted those bones! It worked. Bill and Tom, Shep and Pete were all ready to race.

On race day Bill got a big bone with meat on it for Shep and a small bone with meat on it for Pete. The boys had to think of one more thing. How would they show the bone to the dogs with all the other pets, boys, and girls there? They put the bones in bags. When the race started, Bill and Tom stood by the end line and took the bones out of the bags. ALL the dogs saw the bones and ran to Bill and Tom! Shep and Pete ran like the wind. Both dogs got there before the rest of the dogs. They both got the bones, but Shep won the race. Pete was not the fastest dog today.   The other kids had treats for their dogs too but did not like that Bill and Tom's dogs won. They made a rule that no kid could show a treat when the dogs ran the race. Kids had to give the dogs a treat when the race was over.

Leveled Reading Passage 3

<u>Story 3: Beth and Opal Want a Pet</u>   early to mid 2nd grade

	Line	Words Per Paragraph	Total
Beth lives at the end of the block. Opal lives across the street.	13	13	13
The street is not busy with cars, so they cross to each other's home a lot.	16	29	29
They play almost every day. When it is warm outside, they like to be	14	43	43
outside.	1	44	44
Beth and Opal do not have pets. They both want a pet, but their	14	14	58
moms and dads say they must prove they can take care of a pet. But	15	29	73
how can they prove they can take care of a pet when they do not have	16	45	89
one to take care of?	5	50	94
They are both ten and in the fifth grade. What can they do? 13	13	107	
They can ask for help from other kids. They can ask mom and dad to tell	16	29	123
them how they can prove they can take care of a pet or think up ideas	16	45	139
on their own. Both of their moms and dads tell them to think about	14	59	153
what they need to do to take care of a pet. Beth's mom says "no pet hair	17	76	170
in the house." Opal's mom says, "no pet smells in the house." Both	13	89	183
moms say, "no pet messes and no scratches on things inside the house."	14	103	197
This seems like no pets at all to Beth and Opal!	11	114	208
Beth and Opal sit down in the grass in the front yard at Opal's home.	15	15	223
They are looking very sad. Soon Mr. Joe, who lives at the other end of	15	30	238
the block comes by. He is walking his dog, Jake. He hears Beth say it is	16	51	254
no use. She says they will not have a chance to show mom and dad they	16	67	270
can take care of a pet. This gives Mr. Joe an idea. He is going on a trip	18	85	288
soon. Beth and Opal can take care of Jake at his home when he is gone.	17	102	305
He will be gone for three days. Beth and Opal say they will ask their	15	117	320
moms and dads. Mr. Joe tells them that he will show them what to do	15	132	335
and how to get into his home so they can take care of Jake.	14	146	349
When they ask their moms and dads, they all say "yes." So later that	14	14	363
day they go to see Mr. Joe. He shows them how to push the buttons to	16	30	379
unlock the door. He tells them about Jake's food and gives Jake his food	14	44	393
and water in front of them. He shows them where to find the leash. He	15	59	408
says Jake will want to take a walk in the morning, at noon and again	15	74	423
after supper each day. He tells them to use bags by the back door to	15	89	438
pick up after Jake each time they walk him. Jake is a good dog so he	16	105	454
will not make a mess in the house. But, after the last walk of the day	16	121	470
he must get in his cage. He will feel safer there with Mr. Joe gone.	15	136	485
The day comes for Mr. Joe to leave. Beth and Opal do everything Mr.	14	150	499

Story 3: Beth and Opal Want a Pet

early to mid 2nd grade

	Line	Words Per Paragraph	Total
Joe says to do. Opal walks Jake first. Beth gives Jake food and water.	14	164	513
At noon Beth walks Jake and Opal goes too. Later Opal walks Jake	13	177	526
again, and Beth puts him in his cage. They both pick up after Jake.	14	191	540
They both do not like to pick up after Jake, but they do the job they	16	207	556
have to do. Mr. Joe comes home three days later. He is happy that	14	221	570
Jake has had good care. He tells Beth and Opal's moms and dads	13	234	583
that they are good pet moms. Now Beth and Opal hope they can have	14	248	597
pets, but they still do not know what kind of pets they want! What	14	262	603
kind of pet do you think they should have?	9	271	611

Story 3: Beth and Opal Want a Pet

Beth lives at the end of the block. Opal lives across the street. The street is not busy with cars, so they cross to each other's home a lot. They play almost every day. When it is warm outside, they like to be outside.

Beth and Opal do not have pets. They both want a pet, but their moms and dads say they must prove they can take care of a pet. But how can they prove they can take care of a pet when they do not have one to take care of?

They are both ten and in the fifth grade. What can they do? They can ask for help from other kids. They can ask mom and dad to tell them how they can prove they can take care of a pet or think up ideas on their own.

Both of their moms and dads tell them to think about what they need to do to take care of a pet. Beth's mom says, "no pet hair in the house." Opal's mom says, "no pet smells in the house." Both moms say" no pet messes and no scratches on things inside the house." This seems like no pets at all to Beth and Opal!

Beth and Opal sit down in the grass in the front yard at Opal's home.

They are looking very sad. Soon Mr. Joe, who lives at the other end of the block, comes by. He is walking his dog, Jake. He hears Beth say it is no use. She says they will not have a chance to show mom and dad they can take care of a pet. This gives Mr. Joe an idea. He is going on a trip soon. Beth and Opal can take care of Jake at his home when he is gone. He will be gone for three days.

Beth and Opal say they will ask their moms and dads. Mr. Joe tells them that he will show them what to do and how to get into his home so they can take care of Jake.

When they ask their moms and dads, they all say "yes." So later that day they go to see Mr. Joe. He shows them how to push the buttons to unlock the door. He tells them about Jake's food and gives Jake his food and water in front of them. He shows them where to find the leash. He says Jake will want to take a walk in the morning, at noon and again after supper each day. He tells them to use bags by the back door to pick up after Jake each time they walk him. Jake is a good dog so he will not make a mess in the house. But, after the last walk of the day he must get in his cage. He will feel safer there with Mr. Joe gone.

The day comes for Mr. Joe to leave. Beth and Opal do everything

Mr. Joe says to do. Opal walks Jake first. Beth gives Jake food and water. At noon Beth walks Jake and Opal goes too. Later Opal walks Jake

again, and Beth puts him in his cage. They both pick up after Jake. They both do not like to pick up after Jake, but they do the job they have to do.

   Mr. Joe comes home three days later. He is happy that Jake has had good care. He tells Beth and Opal's moms and dads that they are good pet moms. Now Beth and Opal hope they can have pets, but they still do not know what kind of pets they want! What kind of pet do you think they should have?

Story 4: Can We Go on a Summer Trip? — Late 2nd Grade Early 3rd Grade

	Words Per Sentence	Words Per Paragraph	Words Per Story
Tom is going on a trip with his mom and dad. They like to see	15	15	15
places where things happened a long time ago. This time they want to	13	28	28
see a town by a river that is more than 200 years old. The town is	16	44	44
called Marietta. It is in Ohio. The homes and hotel are very old. There	15	59	59
will be people wearing old clothes and acting like people did 200 years ago.	14	73	73
This year, Tom's mom and dad said that Tom could ask Bill to go	14	14	87
with them, but first Bill's mom and dad had to say yes. Bill lives with his	16	20	103
mom but his dad lives across town. Bill visits his dad on Tuesday and	14	34	117
Saturday some weeks, and other weeks, he sees him on Wednesday and	12	46	129
Sunday. This is because his dad's work hours change each week. If Bill	13	59	142
goes on a trip with Tom, he may miss seeing his dad for a week or two.	17	76	159
His dad may not like that.	6	82	165
Bill and Tom made a plan to tell Bill's dad about the trip in such a	16	16	181
way that his dad would not want to say no. Tom got some pictures of the	16	32	197
things they would see. There were pictures of men in clothes from 1776.	13	45	210
There was a picture of the father of our country. Bill had a picture of a	16	61	226
buggy, boats, and a barge. He also had a picture of a bridge going across	15	76	241
the Ohio river. He got a picture of the old hotel they would stay in. It	16	92	257
was shaped like a triangle.	5	97	262
Bill was ready to tell his dad about the trip. Bill showed them to	14	14	276
his dad. Tom went with him that day. Bill's dad saw the pictures and how	15	29	291
much Bill wanted to go and see these things. He saw that he would not	15	44	306
see Bill for one week, but said it was okay. He wanted Bill to have fun on	17	61	323
a trip with Tom. Bill's mom said it was just fine too.	12	73	335
Bill and Tom were glad and told Tom's mom and	10	10	345
dad. They could not wait for the trip to start!	10	20	355

Story 4: Can We Go on a Summer Trip?

Tom is going on a trip with his mom and dad. They like to see places where things happened a long time ago. This time they want to see a town by a river that is more than 200 years old. The town is called Marietta. It is in Ohio. The homes and hotel are very old. There will be people wearing old clothes and acting like people did 200 years ago.

This year, Tom's mom and dad said that Tom could ask Bill to go with them, but first Bill's mom and dad had to say yes. Bill lives with his mom and his dad lives across town. Bill visits his dad on Tuesday and Saturday some weeks and other weeks he sees him on Wednesday and Sunday. This is because his dad's work hours change each week. If Bill goes on a trip with Tom, he may miss seeing his dad for a week or two. His dad may not like that.

Bill and Tom made a plan to tell Bill's dad about the trip in such a way that his dad would not want to say no. Tom got some pictures of the things they would see. There were pictures of men in clothes from 1776. There was a picture of the father of our country. Bill had a picture of a buggy, boats, and a barge. He also had a picture of a bridge going across the Ohio river. He got a picture of the old hotel they would stay in. It was shaped like a triangle.

Bill was ready to tell his dad about the trip. Bill showed them to his dad. Tom went with him that day. Bill's dad saw the pictures and how much Bill wanted to go and see these things. He saw that he would not see Bill for one week, but said it was okay. He wanted Bill to have fun on a trip with Tom. Bill's mom said it was just fine too.

Bill and Tom were glad and told Tom's mom and dad. They could not wait for the trip to start!

Story 5:   Going on a Trip   Late 4th grade – Early 5th grade

		Words Per	
	Line	Paragraph	Story

Today was the last day in June, the first day of the big trip. Tom and Bill | 17 | 17 | 17

were ready to go. First thing in the morning they went to Perkin's diner | 14 | 31 | 31

for breakfast. After they left Richmond, they drove to Ohio. They saw | 12 | 43 | 43

Dayton, but did not stop. Next, they drove past Xenia. Then they drove to | 14 | 57 | 57

Circleville. After that, they went to Logan and stopped outside of the | 12 | 69 | 69

town. | 1 | 70 | 70

   In Logan Tom's dad said they were stopping to see Old Man's Cave. | 13 | 13 | 83

Bill and Tom did not know about this stop. It was time to eat and Tom's | 16 | 29 | 99

Mom had made a picnic. After Tom's dad parked the car; they ate lunch | 14 | 43 | 113

under a big tree. | 4 | 47 | 117

   Next, they walked down the hill to the path that went down to the cave. | 15 | 15 | 132

The boys could not believe what they saw. There was a huge open spot | 14 | 29 | 146

that went down, down, down rock steps into an open cave. A waterfall | 13 | 42 | 159

and small creek flowed at the bottom. There was a rock footbridge and | 13 | 55 | 172

a tunnel carved into the rocks. Ferns and cedar trees were growing all | 13 | 68 | 185

around. | 1 | 69 | 186

    Tom's dad told them the story about an old man that had lived | 13 | 13 | 199

in the cave for many years. He had carved the tunnel and made the bridge | 15 | 28 | 214

He had carved the steps. | 6 | 34 | 220

   After hiking the cave, they got back into the car. The next stop was | 14 | 14 | 234

Marietta. The boys could not wait to see the Ohio river, hear about how | 14 | 28 | 248

the founding fathers, who settled the area and split up the land, | 12 | 40 | 260

had lived in the early 1800s. | 6 | 46 | 266

   At the hotel they rode up a very old lift to the next floor. Their room had | 17 | 17 | 283

a porch that set up high above ground. They could see very far across the | 15 | 32 | 298

Ohio river. They saw barges pushing boats with piles of coal. They saw | 13 | 45 | 311

power boats racing and cabin boats cruising. | 7 | 52 | 318

   After they got all their things inside the hotel, they went to ride in a | 15 | 15 | 333

little, open bus to see the town. They found out that the town was a fort | 16 | 31 | 349

and one of the first places settled in Ohio. Many of the men that founded | 15 | 46 | 364

the town were officers in the Revolutionary War. The men came because | 12 | 58 | 376

they were paid with land grants in Ohio for fighting the war. Tom and Bill | 15 | 73 | 391

saw a man wearing clothes from that time measuring land. They learned | 12 | 85 | 403

that the men had marked the land so parts of it could be given to | 15 | 100 | 418

each man. Today when people own land in Ohio, they get papers that | 13 | 113 | 431

tell the name of each person whoever had that land. The paper tells | 13 | 126 | 444

Story 5:   Going on a Trip   Late 4th grade – Early 5th grade

	Words Per		
	Line	Paragraph	Story
which man was the first to own that land. The markers are still in	14	140	458
place to this day.	4	144	462
Later Tom and Bill saw two big buildings full of things from those days	14	14	476
They saw old guns, knives, and clothes They saw old tools used by.	13	27	489
hunters, doctors, and people in their homes. They saw real log homes	12	39	501
and saw how people lived inside.	6	45	507
Soon the trip was over, and it was time to go home. The boys had	15	15	522
a goodtime. Now in class when they hear about how brave men	12	27	534
lived and fought so we could be free today, the class will mean	13	40	547
more to them. Now they think about how lucky they are to have	13	53	560
the freedom to do the things they can do. Their country is free	13	66	573
all because of how others long, long, ago fought and worked	11	77	584
hard to make plans so we might have freedom in our country today.	13	90	597

Story 5: Going on a Trip

Today was the last day in June, the first day of the big trip. Tom and Bill were ready to go. First thing in the morning they went to Perkin's for breakfast. After they left Richmond, they drove to Ohio. They saw Dayton but did not stop. Next, they drove past Xenia. Then they drove to Circleville. After that, they went to Logan and stopped outside of the town.

In Logan Tom's dad said they were stopping to see Old Man's Cave. Bill and Tom did not know about this stop. It was time to eat, and Tom's mom had made a picnic. After Tom's dad parked the car, they ate lunch under a big tree.

Next, they walked down the hill to the path that went down to the cave. The boys could not believe what they saw. There was a huge open spot that went down, down, down rock steps into an open cave. A waterfall and small creek flowed at the bottom. There was a rock footbridge and a tunnel carved into the rocks. Ferns and cedar trees were growing all around.

Tom's dad told them the story about an old man that had lived in the cave for many years. He had carved the tunnel and made the bridge. He had carved the steps.

After hiking the cave, they got back into the car. The next stop was Marietta. The boys could not wait to see the Ohio river, hear about how the founding fathers, who settled the area and split up the land, had lived in the early 1800s.

At the hotel they rode up a very old lift to the next floor. Their room had a porch that set up high above ground. They could see very far across the Ohio river. They saw barges pushing boats with piles of coal. They saw power boats racing and cabin boats cruising.

After they got all their things inside the hotel, they went to ride in a little, open bus to see the town. They found out that the town was a fort and one of the first places settled in Ohio. Many of the men that founded the town were officers in the Revolutionary War. The men came because they were paid with land grants in Ohio for fighting the war. Tom and Bill saw a man wearing clothes from that time measuring land. They learned that the men had marked the land so parts of it could be given to each man. Today when people own land in Ohio, they get papers that tell the name of each person whoever had that land. The paper tells which man was the first to own that land. The markers are still in place to this day.

Later Tom and Bill saw two big buildings full of things from those days. They saw old guns, knives, and clothes. They saw old tools used by hunters, doctors, and people in their homes. They saw real log homes and saw how people lived inside.

Soon the trip was over, and it was time to go home. The boys had a goodtime. Now in class, when they hear about how brave men lived and fought so we could be free today, the class will mean more to them. Now they think about how lucky they are to have the freedom to do the things they can do. Their country is free all because of how others long, long, ago fought and worked hard to make plans so we might have freedom in our country today.

Repeated Reading Chart

120						
117						
114						
111						
108						
105						
102						
99						
96						
93						
90						
87						
84						
81						
78						
75						
72						
69						
66						
63						
60						
57						
54						
51						
48						
45						
42						
39						
36						
33						
30						
27						
24						
21						
18						
15						
12						
9						
6						
3						
Date						
# errors						
Story Title						
Story Level						

Is Eddy At Uncle Ollie's?

CCVC DELETIONS TABLE

NAME_____

DATE:_____ DEL._____ SEG._____ BLEND_____ INS._____

Name _____ Date #1 _____ Date #2 _____

Word	Deletion	Segment	Blend	Insertion	Word	Deletion	Segment	Blend	Insertion
1 black					1 froze				
2 black					2 fred				
3 flag					3 pride				
4 frog					4 pray				
5 plate					5 train				
6 blast					6 trade				
7 slip					7 drink				
8 sleek					8 drip				
9 clean					9 great				
10 climb lime					10 crave				

Date #3 _____ Date #4 _____

Word	Deletion	Segment	Blend	Insertion
1 dream				
2 stop				
3 slade				
4 slim				
5 speak				
6 spill				
7 smell				
8 smile				
9 snow				
10 sneeze				

CCVC DELETIONS TABLE ANSWERS

NAME_____ DATE:_____ DEL._____ SEG._____ BLEND_____ INS._____

Name: _____ Date #1: _____ Date #2: _____ Date #3: _____ Date #4: _____

Word	Deletion	Segment	Blend	Insertion	Word	Deletion	Segment	Blend	Insertion	Word	Deletion	Segment	Blend	Insertion
1 block	lock				1 froze	roze				1 stream	team/ seam			
2 black	lack				2 fried	ried/ried				2 stop	top/sop			
3 flag	lag				3 pride	ride				3 slide	lied/side			
4 frog	rog/fog				4 pray	ray/pay				4 slim	limb			
5 place	race/pace				5 train	rain				5 speak	peak/seek			
6 blaid	laid/laid				6 trade	rad				6 spill	pill/sill			
7 help	elp/hep				7 drink	rink				7 small	sall/mall			
8 sleek	leak/seek				8 drip	dia/rip				8 smile	mile			
9 clean	lean/leen				9 great	rate/gate				9 grow	no/know row/row			
10 climb	lime				10 grave	rave/cave				10 sneeze	knees /sees			

DELETION TABLE CVCC

Name _____ Date _____ #1 _____ #2 _____ #3 _____

Word	Deletion	Segment	Blend	Insertion	Word	Deletion	Segment	Blend	Insertion	Word	Deletion	Segment	Blend	Insertion
1.bend					1.belt					1.clamp				
2.bold					2.mast					2.cramp				
3.cond					3.west					3.clamp				
4.mild					4.left					4.bunch				
5.board					5.last					5.lisp				
6.plaid					6.pest					6.pump				
7.field					7.melt					7.tramp				
8.child					8.mist					8.limp				
9.send					9.went					9.dusk				
10.fend					10.dent					10.lamp				

CVCC DELETIONS TABLE ANSWERS

DATE: _____ DEL. _____ SEG. _____ BLEND _____ INS. _____

NAME _____

Name:					Date #1:					Date #2:				
Word	Deletion	Segment	Blend	Insertion	Word	Deletion	Segment	Blend	Insertion	Word	Deletion	Segment	Blend	Insertion
1 bend	ben/bed				1 bolt	boll / bet				1 damp	dam			
2 bald	bolt				2 malt	mass / mot				2 cramp	cram			
3 kord	kore/kode				3 vest	ves/vet				3 klamp	clam/clap			
4 mild	mile				4 left	let				4 bunch	bun			
5 board	bore				5 lest	less				5 lop	lip			
6 pled	paid/paid				6 pest	pet				6 plump	lad			
7 held	hold				7 melt	mest/Met				7 tramp	top			
8 child	chide				8 mrst	mrsy/mrtt				8 limp	limb			
9 send	sod				9 vent	when/wet				9 dusk	duck			
10 blend	lent/led				10 dent	delt/den				10 lamp	lamb			

Date #3: _____ Date #4: _____

CORRECTLY SPELLED WORDS SPELLING CHART

CORRECTLY SPELLED WORDS SPELLING CHART
Each column equals one word.
Color one box for each word correctly spelled

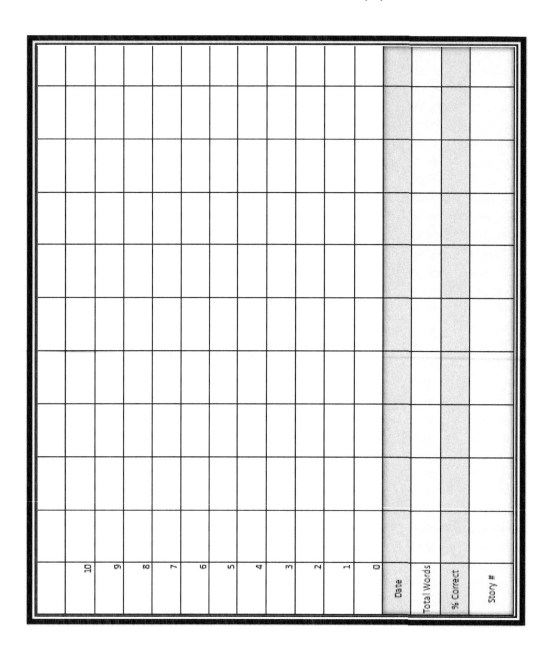

Graph Paper

When to use 'c' or 'k

For many children the letter 'c' is confusing. It is 'interchangeable' with the letters 'k' and 's.' Therefore, how can they know which letter to choose when writing words containing the /k/ sound?

Here are some guidelines that, although are not absolute every time, are reliable for most words having the 'k' sound.

Rules for the letters 'c' and 'k'

1. Usually, words having the initial /s/ just before the letters 'I' 'e' or 'y' will begin with the letter 's' instead of the letter 's'---but not always.
2. Where the first sound is /s/ and the next letter is 'a' 'o' 'u' or another consonant, the first letter will be 's'.
3. When the sound /k/ begins a word and the second letter is 'I' 'e' or 'y', then the /k/ sound will be the letter 'k'. Why? Because the letters 'I' 'e' and 'y' turn the letter 'c' into the /s/ sound.
4. When the first sound is /k/ and the second letter is 'a' 'o' 'u' or another consonant, then the first letter will be 'c

1.	2.	3.	4.	5.
city	such	kite	code	class
cell	sad	keep	calm	crock
center	sack	kiss	cord	crop
cygnet	sand	kid	calm	cross
ceiling	sort	kept	cake	crow
celery	sore	Ken	clam	climb
certain	sole	kind	core	clock
cede	sob	key	cop	cliff
seal	sort	king	cope	create
seed	sank	kick	cape	crab
sick	sang	kit	case	crumb
sip	sue	Kyle	cost	clip
sill	sags	kin	curl	close
sell	saw	kiwi	cuts	crisp

ee	ee	ee	i	i	i	e	e	e
ae	a	a	a	u	u	u	o	o
o	oe	oo	oo	ue	ie	oy	oi	ou
ow	au	aw	oa	ough	igh	eigh	ea	dge
ai	ew	ui	ey	ay	ei	ea	oul	tch
sh	sh	ch	ch	th	th	ng	ph	ck
kn	gn	qu	mb	wh	wr	ir	ur	zz
er	ar	or	ear	b	b	c	c	z
d	d	f	f	g	g	h	h	y
j	j	k	k	l	l	m	m	y
n	n	p	p	qu	q	r	r	x
s	s	ss	t	t	v	v	w	w

'b' or 'd'?

How can I tell lower case 'b' from lower case d'? /b/ or /d/?

The trick is to use what
you feel

with what you hear

AND what you SEE

When I make the /p/ or the /b/ sounds

My lips press together to form a line
first.

THEN air pops out to make a sound. /b/

Match what you see to what you FEEL when you READ.

When you see a line first, THEN make a line with your lips first to make the sound /b/.

When you see the circle first [it looks like a bubble] then touch your tongue up
/d/ to tap on the bubble.

Match what you FEEL to what you hear when you WRITE.

When you FEEL your lips press together when you make the sound,
then draw the line first and then the circle../b/ = 'b'

When you feel your tongue touch up when you make the sound,
draw the circle first and the line last. /d/ = 'd'

WHEN TO USED -ED ON THE END OF A WORD. IS IT <u>STILL</u> A WORD?

Is it STILL a Word? When you see an ending, say the word without the ending. Is I still a word? If it is, then add a different ending.

For example, held | | this does not have an ending. You will not do anything with this word. This word come from the word "hold." It is an irregular verb. That means it is an action word because you can **hold** things. But, instead of saying **holded**, the word changes to **held** when you already DID the holding.

I hold my bunny.
I am holding my bunny.
Yesterday, I held my bunny.

Could | this does not have an ending. It is not an action word. You will not do anything with this word.

Chirp | this does not have an ending. It is an 'action' word. Birds do this. Add an ending to make it either **chirped** or **chirping.**

Folded | this has an ending [-ed]. The word is **fold** without the ending.   You can take the [-ed] off and add an 'ing' to make the word **folding**. Now you have a new word that means the same thing except the ending tells WHEN you did it.

Jumping | this has and ending [-ing]. The word without the ending is **jump**. Add an -ed, and the word becomes **jumped**.   Again, it means almost the same thing, except the ending tells WHEN you did it.

The following words do not have endings. Can you add one? How is it spelled? On another sheet of paper write each word two times but add a past tense [-ed] and a present tense ending [-ing] if appropriate to each word.

[ex: type   typed   typing]   REMEMBER: change the letter 'y' to an 'I' when adding an ending!

stomp	host	melt	fry
list	what	mild	call
chill	chide	play	cry
chime	old	bloom	try
land	mode	dream	pry
pack	sift	brave	lick
shirt	pull	bright	smash
yield	lift	float	spell
frost	peck	open	listen

/OY/ AND /OI/

boil	foil	soil	toil	join	joint	void
choice	moist	voice	noise	boy	toy	soy
joy	alloy	annoy	decoy	enjoy	envoy	

NOTE: On the end of the Word, /oy/ is usually spelled 'oy'. In the middle of the Word, /oi/ is usually spelled 'oi'.

/OU/ AND /OW/

shout	sound	sour	spout	sprout	stout	thousand
amount	bound	blouse	cloud	count	couch	doubt
out	found	flour	foul	hour	mouth	noun
ounce	cow	clown	brown	fowl	owl	town
power	crown	shower	crowd	growl	towel	brow
frown	vow	prowl	down	how	now	

NOTE: There does not seem to be a pattern for the 'ow' spelling for /ow/ -- it is used in the middle and in the end of words.

However, we do not see 'ou' on the end of words.

244

Long Vowels

Long a	Long e	Long i	Long o	Long u
a_e	e_e	i_e	o_e	u_e
ate	Pete	ice	vote	mute
ape	theme	ride	note	cute
case	eve	hide	hope	cube
late	even	file	cope	tune
	delete	time	tone	tube
ai	ee	y	oa	ew
rain	seed	fry	boat	few
pain	feet	by	coat	new
train	keep	fly	soap	dew
trail	meet	sky	road	grew
snail	need	cry	throat	blew
ay	ea	ie	ow	ue
play	each	pie	bow	true
day	read	tie	crow	cue
ray	lead	lie	grow	fuel
say	near	vie	owe	due
pay	teach	plie	low	clue
ei & eigh	y	igh	oe	
rein	pretty	high	toe	
sleigh	happy	right	doe	
eight	comfy	light	roe	
weight	sunny	sight	hoe	
freight	jumpy	sign	foe	
ey	ie	ey	ough	
they	piece	monkey	dough	
survey	thief	key	though	
hey	cookie	turkey	furlough	
prey	brief	valley	although	
obey	bootie	barley	thorough	

Other Vowels

oo - boo	oo-look	oy - toy	ou - loud
oo	oo	oy	ou
too	hook	boy	couch
boo	book	toy	pound
tool	took	soy	round
food	cool	coy	loud
noon	cook	joy	cloud
ou	u	oi	ow
you	pull	oil	clown
through	put	coil	down
recoup	push	boil	town
coupon	full	toil	brown
detour		toilet	owl
ui	ou	aw	au
fruit	should	dawn	fraught
suit	would	fawn	taught
juice	could	lawn	because
cruise		crawl	fault
bruises		yawn	sauce

other ways to spell short vowels

short i	short e	short u
y	ea	u
gym	head	cut
system	lead	sun
cyst	ready	supper
cymbal	tread	up
symphony	bread	under
short o	ai	ou
ough	said	touch
bought		enough
sought		rough
wrought		famous
fought		serious
cough		o
		done
		love
		cover
		does
		color
		from

Is Eddy At Uncle Ollie's?

Short vowels

short i	short e	short a	short u	short o
i	e	a	u	o
sit	bed	hat	fun	spot
pin	red	cat	pun	shop
if	let	can	rush	drop
is	met	gas	hung	soft
with	pet	pass	shut	loft
mit	pen	fan	plug	rock

245

REVERSALS

The ability to listen to two sounds and switch them around in the mind to create a new word is difficult for many children. An awareness of sound, or phoneme, order helps children to correctly order phonemes when writing [spelling] and when reading. The following list of two-phoneme switches may be used with an easy turn-taking game. It is very important that the child NOT see letters, and only hear the phonemes as they THINK about reversing the phonemes to create new words

uth=the

fo = off

sie = ice

oyb = boy

eesh = she

oeg = go

ti = it

ieb = bye

ees = see

eem = me

eat = tea

eeb = be

eep = pea

eef = fee

vee = eve

lee = eel

een = knee

fi = if

zi = is

chi = itch

li = itch

li = ill

ree = ear

ni = in

knaw = on

own = no

eek = key

koa = oak

iet = tie

ire = rye

ied = dye

iep = pie

aed = day

aeth = they

air = ray

ace = say

ache = kay

tea = eat

tay = eight

no = own

day = aid

ray = air

say = ace

I'm = my

ien = nigh

aim = may

ieg = guy

on=know

Phonic Rules Word Lists
FLOSS RULE

toss - toes	sell -seal	stress
bass - base	shell	gloss
bell,	tell - teal	fess
chill	skull	bull
boss	skill	chess -cheese
hill	mess	guess - geese
dull - duel	dress	stuff
pill -pile	glass	scuff
full - fuel	miss - mice	cuff
gull	shall -shale	fluff
loss	moss	bluff
lass- lace	fuss	puff
lull	brass - brace	huff
mull- mule	press	stuff

-ck RULE

back - bake	sock--soak	broke
tack - take	peck--peek	coke
rack - rake	slick	soak
lack – lake	thick	joke
sack – sake	neck	fake
lick – like	deck	cake
tick – tyke	kick	make
Mick – Mike	sick	seek
pick – pike	chick	meek
check – cheek	stick	leak
peck – peek	flick	puke
wreck -- reek	fleck	poke
puck – puke	brick	
duck – Duke	block	
luck – Luke	pluck	

-tch RULE

hatch	hitch	reach
patch	Mitch	beach
match	witch	each
batch	fetch	coach
thatch	notch	poach
latch	scratch	roach
catch	hutch	pooch
pitch	peach	except: rich
ditch	teach	except: which

-dge RULE judge

dodge	sludge	budge
pledge	wedge	ridge
bridge	edge	cage
badge	ledge	wage
lodge	fudge	huge
wedge	stage	page

–le SYLLABLE

purple	paddle	waggle
cradle	tattle	chuckle
little	table	buckle
fiddle	maple	tickle
riddle	staple	cycle

CONSONANT DOUBLING

pull – pulling – pulled	rip –ripping –ripped	holly –holy
fill – filling –filled	fit –fitting –fitted	rudder –ruder
file –filing	like –liking –liked	super –supper
slide – sliding	lick –licking –licked	mopping –moping
ride – riding	fail –failing –failed	fitting –fighting
hop – hopping – hopped	strike- striking	setting – seating
hope –hoping –hoped	dinner –diner	tipping –typing
rope –roping –roped	bitter- biter	

-ce ENDING

ace	ice	dice
face	rice	thrice
pace	mice	slice
race	nice	price

-all ENDING

all	call	fall
small	tall	mall
stall	wall	stall
hall	gall	ball

-old ENDING

cold	mold	bold
sold	hold	fold
old	told	gold

-olt ENDING

bolt	dolt	smolt
jolt	colt	volt

-ose SOUNDS LIKE /z

nose	pose	chose
rose	those	hose

OPEN and CLOSED SYLLABLES

me - met	be - bet	hol-ly – ho-ly
she - shell	we - wet	fil –ling – fi-ling
go - tot	din-ner -- di-ner	hop-ping – ho-ping
a - at	tab –let -- ta-ble	pinned -- pined
so - song	bit-ter – bi –ter	supper -- super

TWO SOUNDS OF –ED

/d/	boated	webbed
weeded	netted	named
wooded	boomed	pinned
needed	beamed	pined
pleaded	dined	whined
noted	tuned	vined

/t/	pooped	topped
whipped	piped	wrapped
wiped	popped	napped

VOWEL DISCRIMINATION WORD LISTS

Word lists that go with:

Is   Eddy   At Uncle   Ollie's?

SHORT VOWEL WORDS: Set 1

1. dig	Ned	pass	mud	top
2. win	wet	man	lug	rob
3. rip	yet	jam	hum	sob
4. thin	Beth	pan	but	dot
5. wish	set	shad	chum	mob
6. ship	led	chap	gut	doll
7. chip	pet	lad	muff	moss
8. with	jet	cat	mud	mop
9. kit	met	sad	tub	jog
10. pit	get	fat	thud	shop

SHORT VOWEL WORDS: Set 2

11. pit	pet	pat	putt	pot
12. pick	peck	pack	puck	pog
13. bit	bet	bat	but	bot
14. bid	bed	bad	bud	bod
15. rid	reg	rag	rub	rock
16. slip	slept	slap	slum	slop
17. pin	pen	pan	pun	pawn
18. did	dead	dad	dud	dock
19. dis c	desk	dash	dust	doss
20. list	lest	last	lust	lost

SHORT VOWEL WORDS: Set 2

1. pit	pet	pat	putt	pot
2. pick	peck	pack	puck	pog
3. bit	bet	bat	but	bot
4. bid	bed	bad	bud	bod
5. rid	reg	rag	rub	rock
6. slip	slept	slap	slum	slop
7. pin	pen	pan	pun	pawn
8. did	dead	dad	dud	dock
9. dis c	desk	dash	dust	doss
10. list	lest	last	lust	lost

LONG AND SHORT VOWEL WORDS IN MINIMAL PAIRS

1. hid/hide	me/meet	mad/made	cut/cute	hop/hope
2. rip/ripe	fed/feed	rat/rate	tub/tube	rob/robe
3. bid/bide	set/seat	at/ate	dud/dude	pop/pope
4. din/dine	led/lead	cap/cape	mutt/mute	nod/node
5. dim/dime	Ned/need	tap/tape	but/butte	rod/rode
6. Tim/time	pep/peep	nap/nape	jut/jute	tot/tote
7. win/wine	fell/feel	Sam/same	just /juice	cop/cope
8. rid/ride	Ken/keen	man/mane	must/moose	call/coal
9. lid/lied	red/reed	pal/pale	dust/deuce	doll/dole
10. kit/kite	wet/wheat	fat/fate	rust/roost	hall/hole

4 KINDS OF SYLLABLES

Open Syllable

me

she

go

I

a

hi

Closed Syllable

met, men

Shell

got, gob

it, ill, in

at, am

hit, hid

Final e Syllable

Pete, seem, meek
Notice that the
'ee' letters like to
stay together

dime, nine

make, male

Luke, mute

vote, cope

-le Syllable

fid dle | ti tle

tem ple | stee ple

wag gle | ta ble

pud dle | pu pil

tog gle | lo cal

to tal

ANSWERS TO CVC WORD LISTS

ANSWERS 1-8

ANSWERS 9-15

ANSWERS 16-22

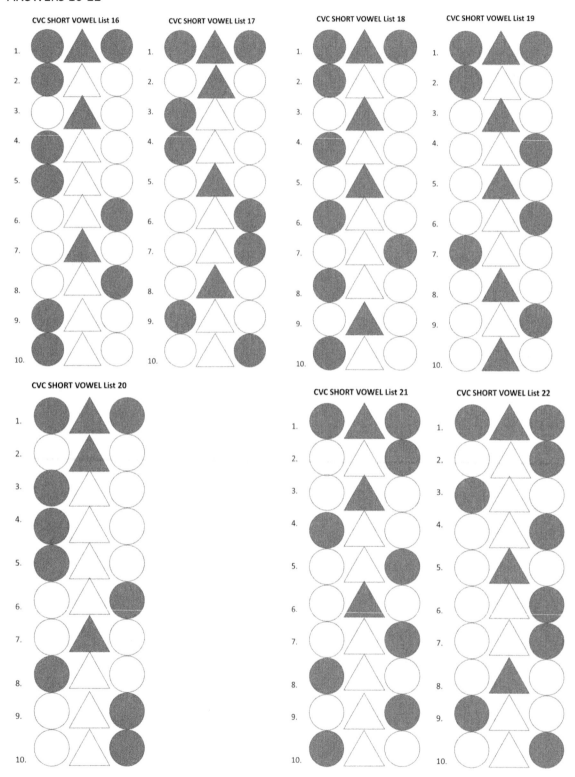

ANSWERS 23-30

ANSWERS 31-38

ANSWERS SHORT VOWEL 39-40 & LONG/SHORT VOWELS 1-4

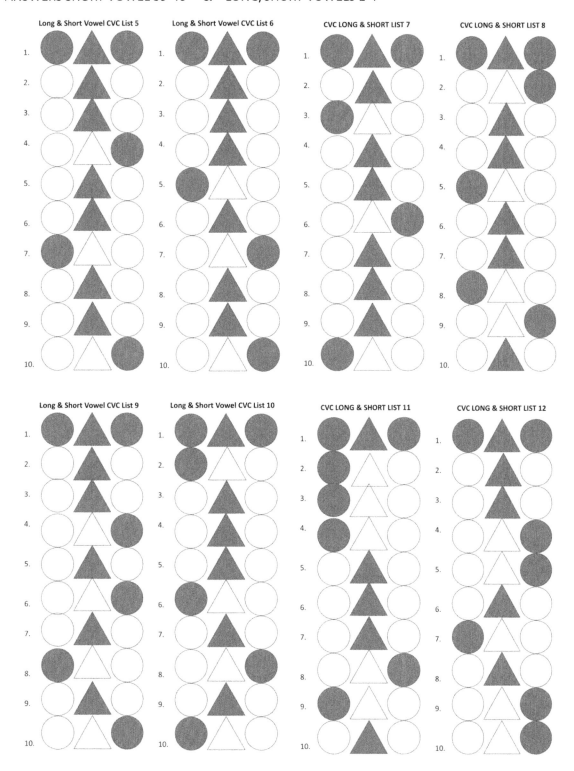

ANSWERS LONG/SHORT 5-12

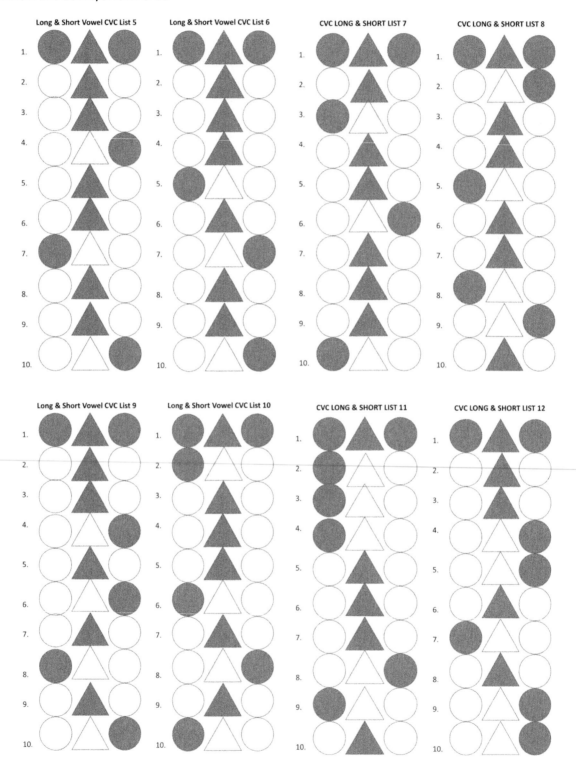

ANSWERS LONG & SHORT 13-19

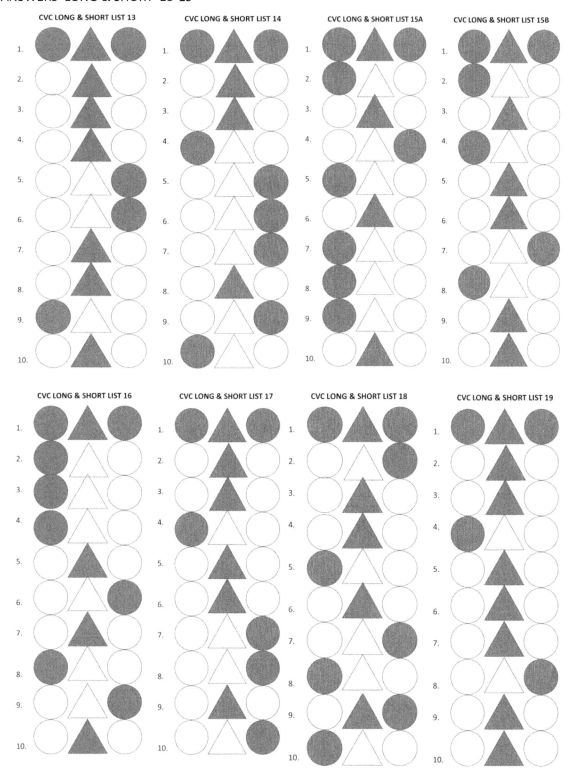

ANSWERS LONG & SHORT 20-27

Winning Solutions for Struggling Readers and Spellers

ANSWERS LONG & SHORT 28-35

263

ANSWERS LONG & SHORT 36-40

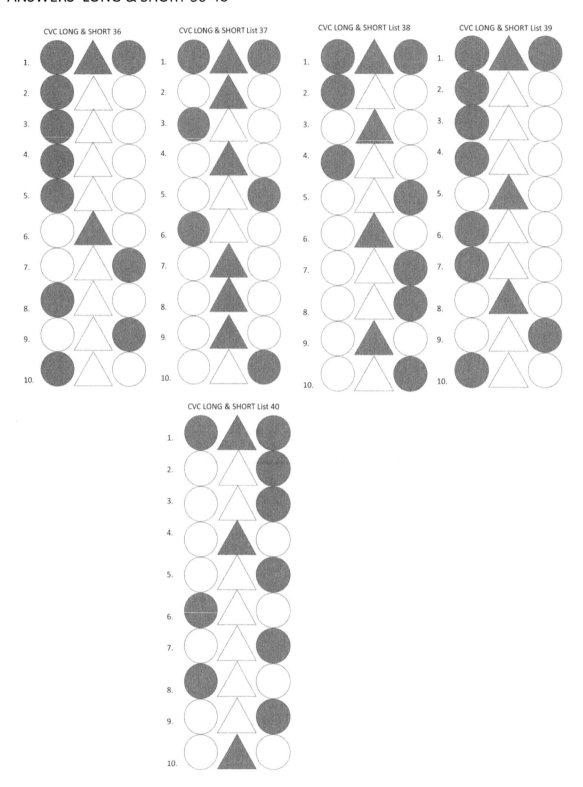

Answers to CCV

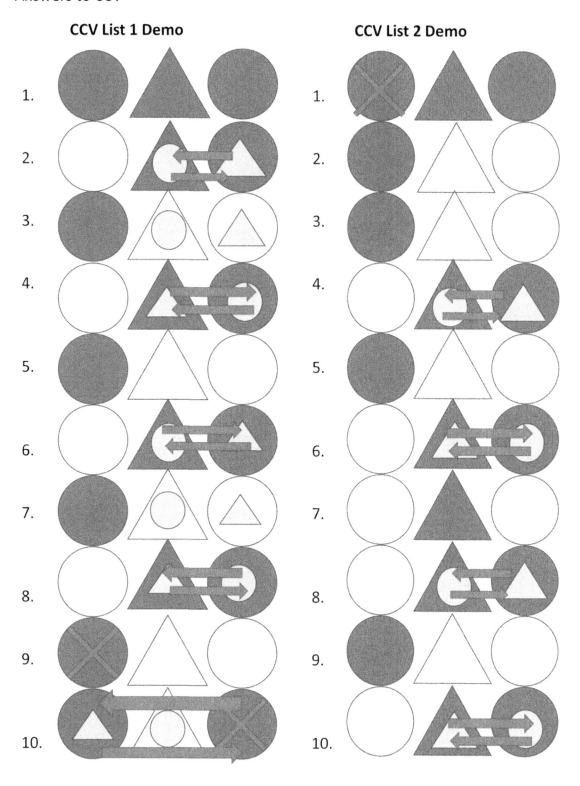

CCV List 1 Demo

CCV List 2 Demo

CCV List 3 Demo

CCV DEMO LIST 4

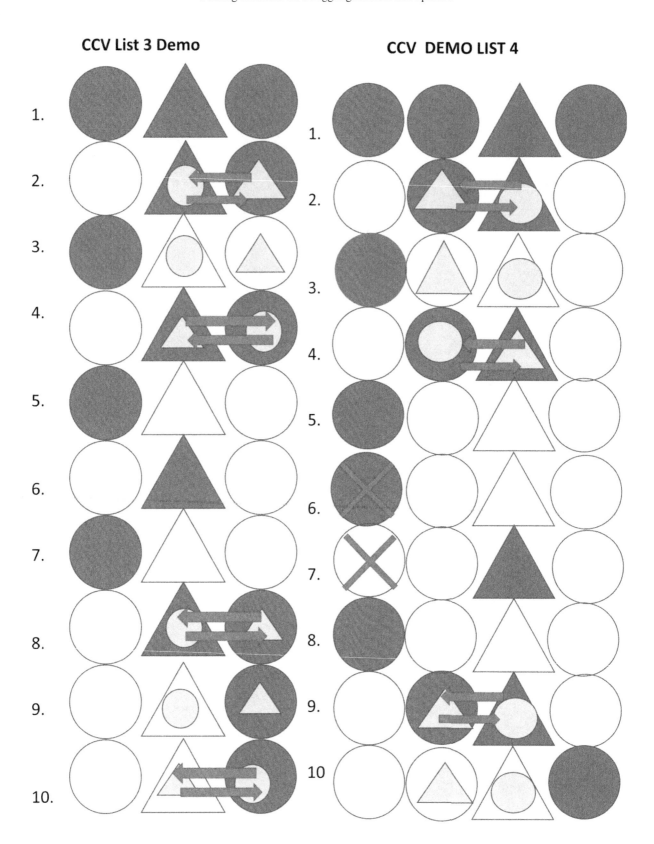

ANSWERS CCV 1-7

ANSWERS CCV 8-10

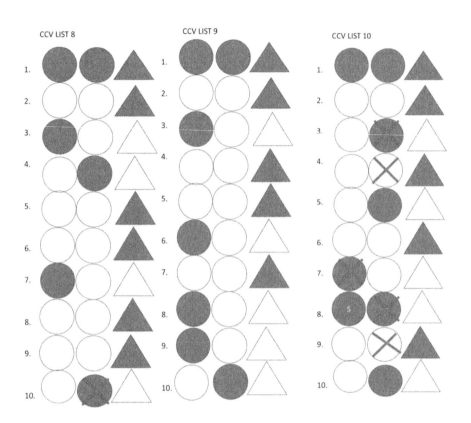

ANSWERS CCVC LIST 11-16

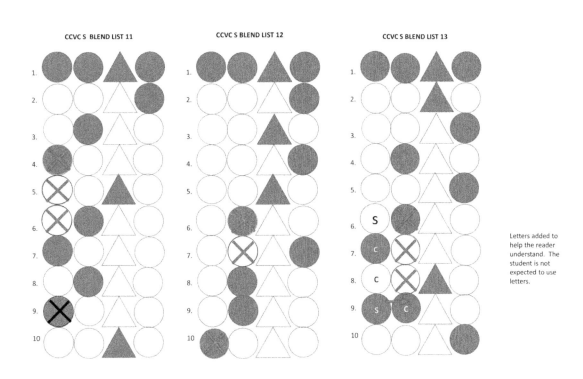

Letters added to help the reader understand. The student is not expected to use letters.

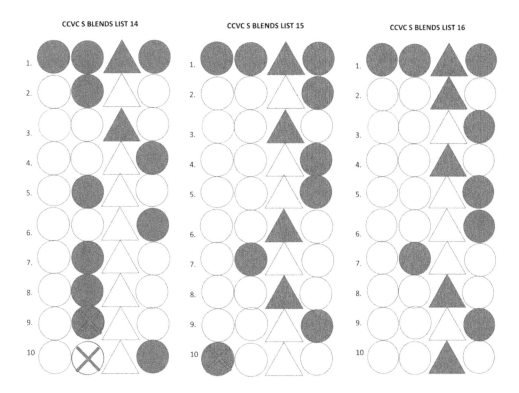

269

ANSWERS CCVC 17-22

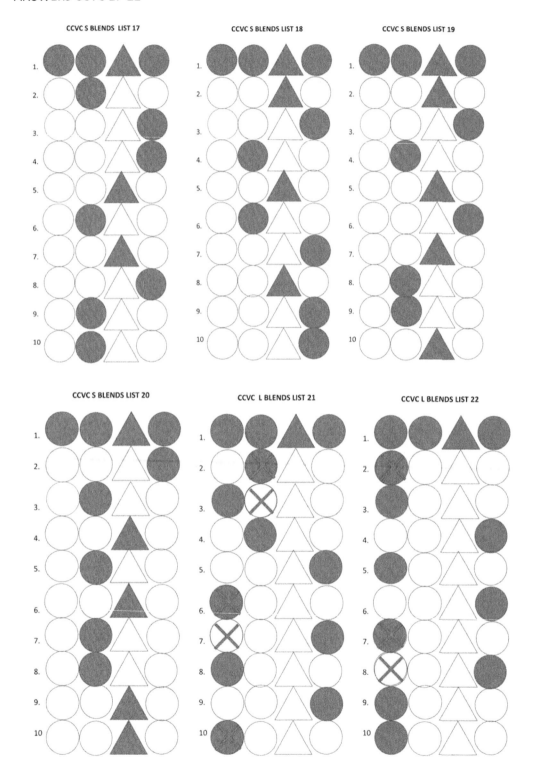

ANSWERS CCVC LIST 23-28

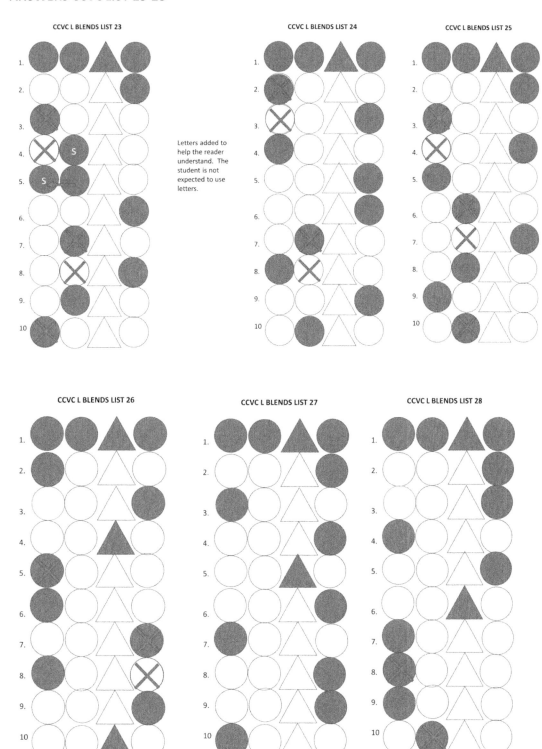

Letters added to help the reader understand. The student is not expected to use letters.

ANSWERS CCVC LIST 29-33

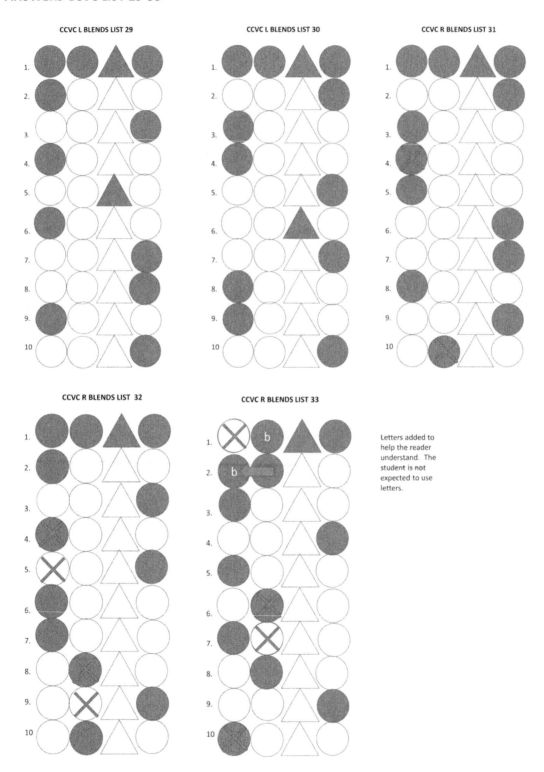

CCVC L BLENDS LIST 29

CCVC L BLENDS LIST 30

CCVC R BLENDS LIST 31

CCVC R BLENDS LIST 32

CCVC R BLENDS LIST 33

Letters added to help the reader understand. The student is not expected to use letters.

ANSWERS CCVC LIST 34-37

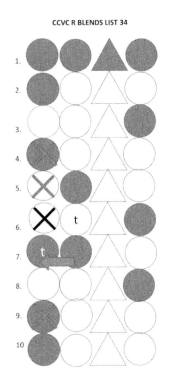

CCVC R BLENDS LIST 34

Letters added to help the reader understand. The student is not expected to use letters.

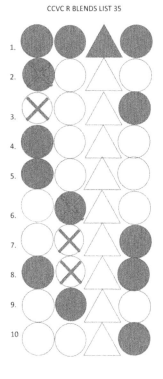

CCVC R BLENDS LIST 35

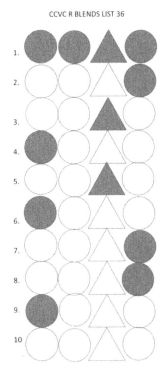

CCVC R BLENDS LIST 36

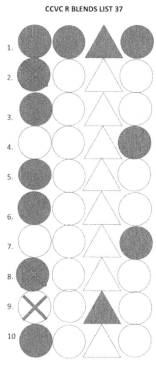

CCVC R BLENDS LIST 37

ANSWERS TO LISTS 38-41

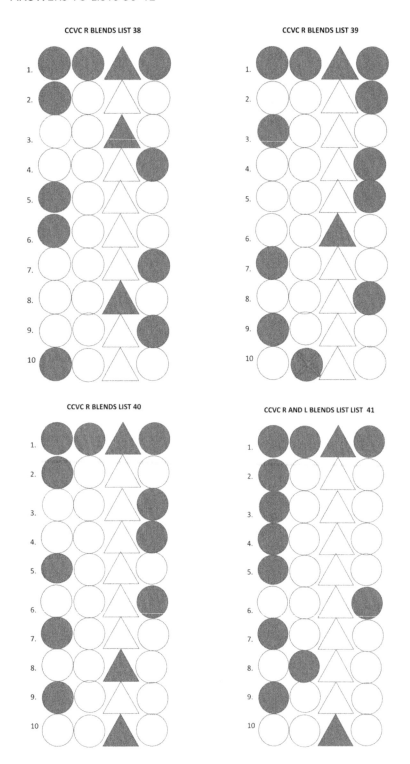

ANSWERS TO LISTS 41-46

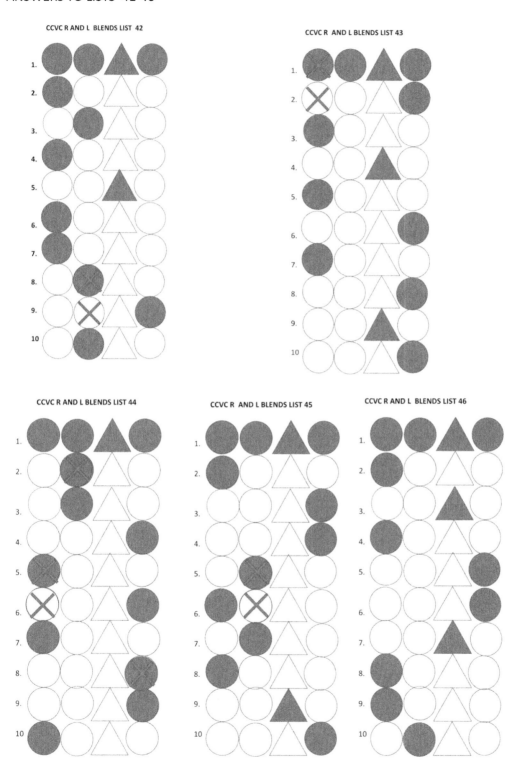

ANSWERS TO LISTS 47-51

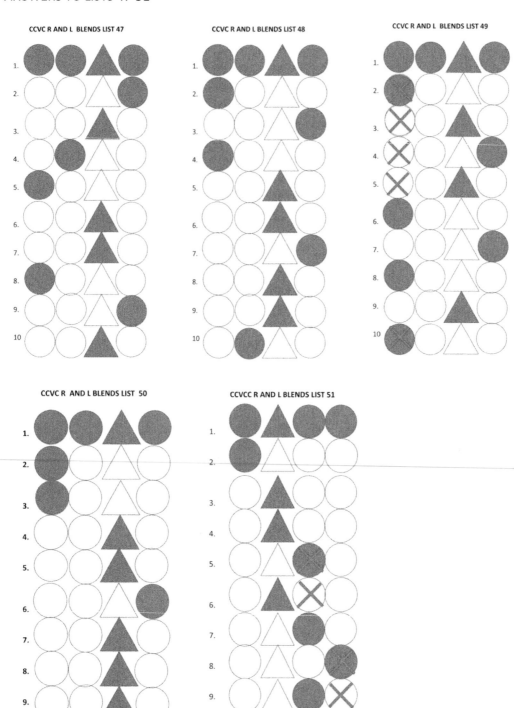

ANSWERS TO LISTS CVCC 52-56

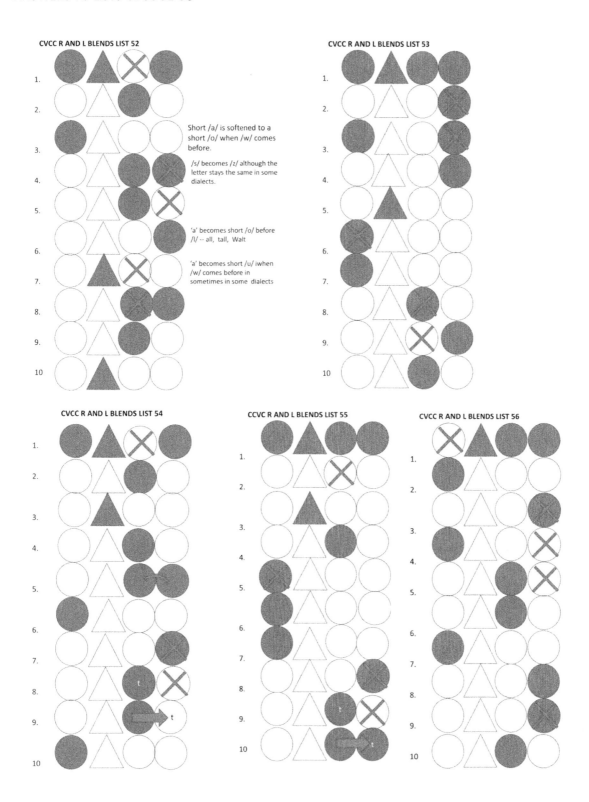

CVCC R AND L BLENDS LIST 52

Short /a/ is softened to a short /o/ when /w/ comes before.

/s/ becomes /z/ although the letter stays the same in some dialects.

'a' becomes short /o/ before /l/ -- all, tall, Walt

'a' becomes short /u/ iwhen /w/ comes before in sometimes in some dialects

CVCC R AND L BLENDS LIST 53

CVCC R AND L BLENDS LIST 54

CCVC R AND L BLENDS LIST 55

CVCC R AND L BLENDS LIST 56

ANSWERS CVCC 57-60

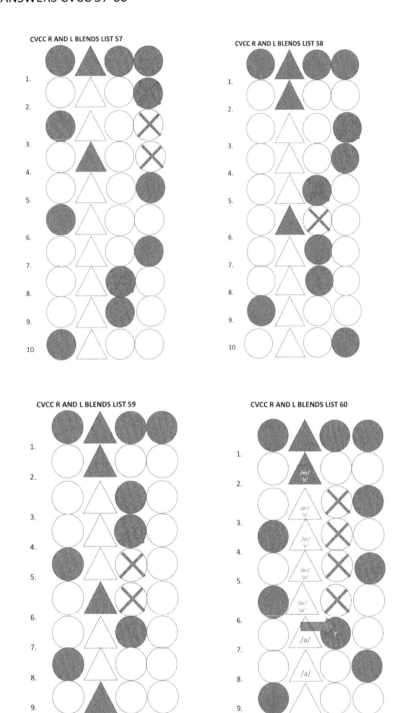

ANSWERS CVCC 61-64

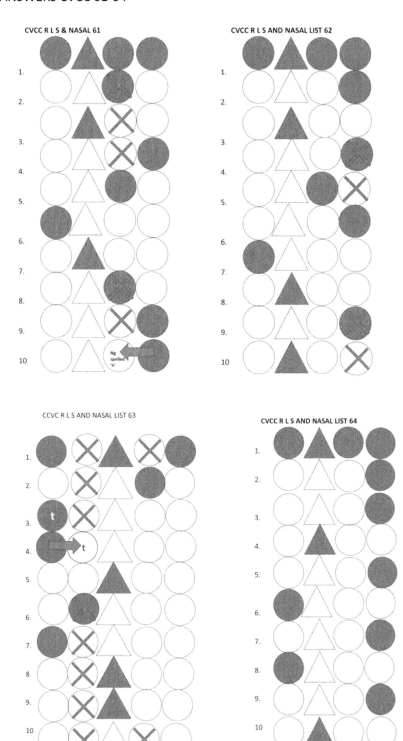

ANSWERS CVCC 65-68

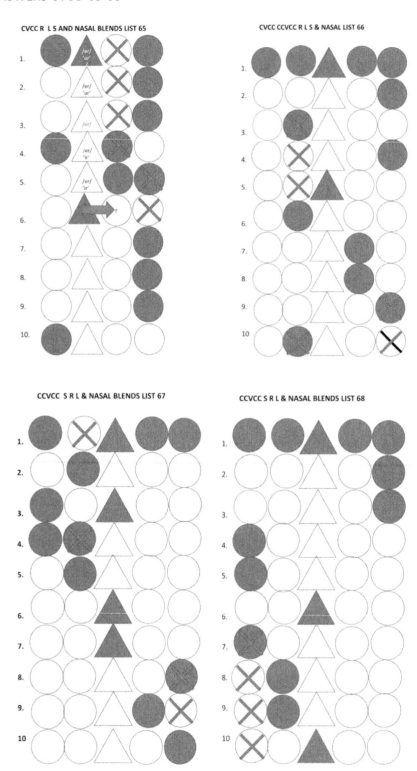

ANSWERS CVCC 69-72

CCVCC S R L & NASAL BLENDS LIST 69

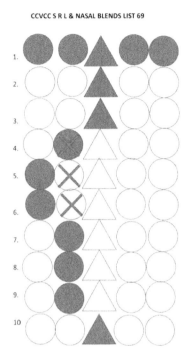

CCVCC S R L & NASAL BLENDS LIST 70

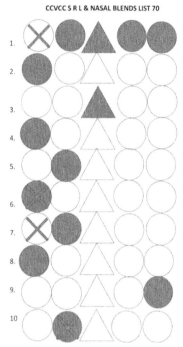

CCVC CVCC CCVCC SH TH CH & R LIST 71

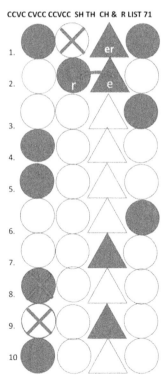

Two mouth movements are made for /ar/ /or/ /ire/ and /ear/

One mouth movement is made for /er/ which can be spelled 'er' 'ir' 'or' AND when the letter 'w' comes before /or/ then it will sound like /er/

Each shape Shows one mouth Movement.

Therefore, we use two shapes for /ar/ /or/ /ire/ & /ear/ sounds but only one shape for /er/ sounds.

CCVC CVCC CCVCC SH TH CH & R LIST 72

Two mouth movements are made for /ar/ /or/ /ire/ and /ear/

One mouth movement is made for /er/ which can be spelled 'er' 'ir' 'or' AND when the letter 'w' comes before /or/ then it will sound like /er/

Each shape Shows one mouth Movement.

Therefore, we use two shapes for /ar/ /or/ /ire/ & /ear/ sounds but only one shape for /er/ sounds.

/P/ /r/ /o/

/P/ /o/ /r/

/p/ /o/ /r/ /ch/

ANSWERS CVCC 73-76

CCVC CVCC CCVCC SH TH CH & R LIST 73

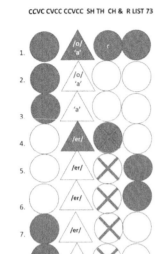

Two mouth movements are made for /ar/ /or/ /ire/ and /ear/

One mouth movement is made for /er/ which can be spelled 'er' 'ir' 'or' AND when the letter 'w' comes before /or/ then it will sound like /er/

Each shape Shows one mouth Movement.

Therefore, we use two shapes for /ar/ /or/ /ire/ & /ear/ sounds but only one shape for /er/ sounds.

CCVC CVCC CCVCC SH TH CH & R LIST 74

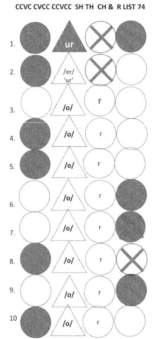

Two mouth movements are made for /ar/ /or/ /ire/ and /ear/

/k/ /o/ /r/ /s/

One mouth movement is made for /er/ which can be spelled 'er' 'ir' 'or' AND when the letter 'w' comes before /or/ then it will sound like /er/

Each shape Shows one mouth Movement.

Therefore, we use two shapes for /ar/ /or/ /ire/ & /ear/ sounds but only one shape for /er/ sounds.

CCVC CVCC CCVCC SH TH CH & R LIST 75

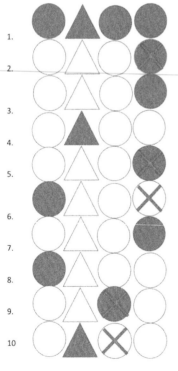

CCVC CVCC CCVCC SH TH CH & R LIST 76

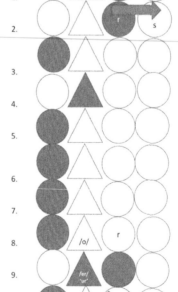

Two mouth movements are made for /ar/ /or/ /ire/ and /ear/

One mouth movement is made for /er/ which can be spelled 'er' 'ir' 'or' AND when the letter 'w' comes before /or/ then it will sound like /er/

Each shape Shows one mouth Movement.

Therefore, we use two shapes for /ar/ /or/ /ire/ & /ear/ sounds but only one shape for /er/ sounds.

ANSWERS CVCC 77-80

CCVC CVCC CCVCC SH TH CH & R LIST 77

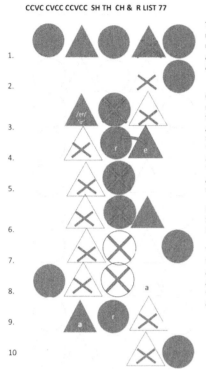

Two mouth movements are made for /ar/ /or/ /ire/ and /ear/

One mouth movement is made for /er/ which can be spelled 'er' 'ir' 'or' AND when the letter 'w' comes before /or/ then it will sound like /er/

Each shape Shows one mouth Movement.

Therefore, we use two shapes for /ar/ /or/ /ire/ & /ear/ sounds but only one shape for /er/ sounds.

CCVC CVCC SH CH TH & R LIST 78

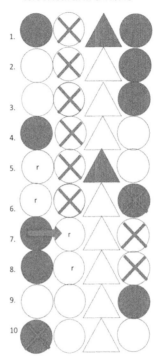

CCVC CVCC SH TH CH & R LIST 79

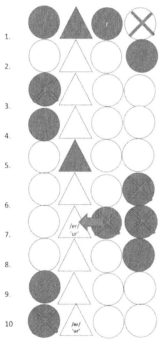

Two mouth movements are made for /ar/ /or/ /ire/ and /ear/

One mouth movement is made for /er/ which can be spelled 'er' 'ir' 'or' AND when the letter 'w' comes before /or/ then it will sound like /er/

Each shape Shows one mouth Movement.

Therefore, we use two shapes for /ar/ /or/ /ire/ & /ear/ sounds but only one shape for /er/ sounds.

CCVC CVCC SH TH CH & R LIST 80

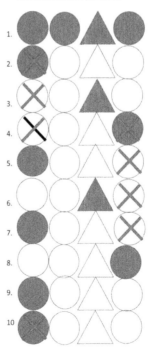

ANSWERS CCV CCVCC CVCC 81-86

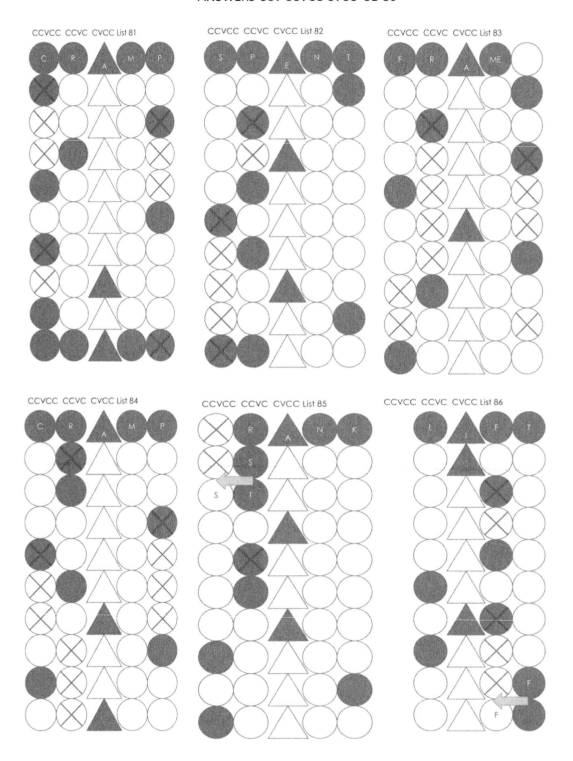

ANSWERS CCVC CCVCC CVCC 87-90

CCVCC CCVC CVCC List 87

CCVCC CCVC CVCC List 88

CCVCC CCVC CVCC List 89

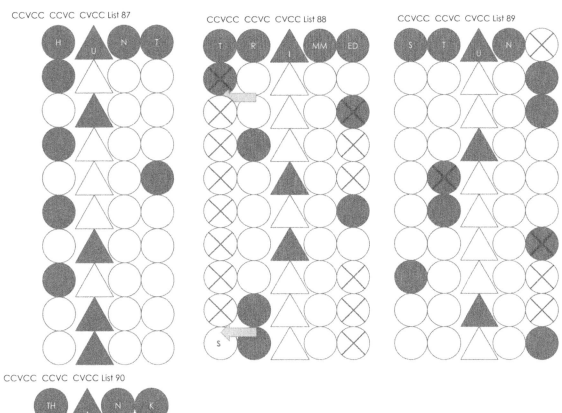

CCVCC CCVC CVCC List 90

Dark ink color is stressed = the stressed syllable. A little louder, longer.

Italicized syllable is the unstressed syllable. Will usually sound like 'uh' and be a little softer and shorter.

<u>Underlined syllable is the suffix, which determines which syllable before it will be stressed and which will be unstressed.</u>

Answers for Multiple Syllable Worksheet 1

ac <u>tion</u>   **sanc** <u>tion</u>

no <u>tion</u>   **sta** <u>tion</u>

cap <u>tion</u>   *a* **dop** <u>tion</u>

fic <u>tion</u>   *pro* **duc** <u>tion</u>

frac <u>tion</u>   *con* **struc** <u>tion</u>

por <u>tion</u>   *af* **fec** <u>tion</u>

junc <u>tion</u>   *in* **fec** <u>tion</u>

ques <u>tion</u>

Answers for Multiple Syllable Worksheet 2

com **ple** tion

se **cre** tion

ex **plo** sion

e **mo** tion

po **si** tion

de **vo** tion

com **mo** tion

dic **ta** tion

fix **a** tion

sen **sa** tion

foun **da** tion

lo **ca** tion

mi **gra** tion

con **di** tion

tra **di** tion

sub **tract** tion

temp **ta** tion

mo *ti* **va** tion

de *vas* **ta** tion

ac *ti* **va** tion

li *ti* **ga** tion

dep *o* **sit** ion

mi *ti* **ga** tion

va *ca* tion

des *per* **a** tion

com *po* **si** tion

ad *mir* **a** tion

mo *ti* **vat** ion

par **ti** tion

con *fis* **ca** tion

com *pe* **ti** tion

pe **ti** tion

ren **di** tion

dis *po* **si** tion

Answers for Multiple Syllable Worksheet 3

vi <u>cious</u>   *con* **ten** <u>tious</u>

in **fec** <u>tious</u>   *vex* **a** <u>tious</u>

fic **ti** <u>tious</u>   *fa* **ce** <u>tious</u>

nu **tri** <u>tious</u>   *pre* **ten** <u>tious</u>

re *pe* **ti** <u>tious</u>   *de* **li** <u>cious</u>

am **bi** <u>tious</u>   **cons** <u>cious</u>

su *per* **sti** <u>tious</u>   *ju* **di** <u>cious</u>

ram **bunc** <u>tious</u>   **gra** <u>cious</u>

ex *pe* **di** <u>tious</u>   **lus** <u>cious</u>

in **fec** <u>tious</u>   *fer* **o** <u>cious</u>

Answers for Multiple Syllable Worksheet 4

ma **jes** <u>tic</u>

a *ca* **dem** <u>ic</u>

al **ler** <u>gic</u>

a *na* **lyt** <u>ic</u>

a *nes* **thet** <u>ic</u>

An **tarc** <u>tic</u>

Pa **cif** <u>ic</u>

At **lan** <u>tic</u>

e *pi* **dem** <u>ic</u>

an *ti* **sep** <u>tic</u>

er **rat** <u>ic</u>

au **then** <u>tic</u>

bo **tan** <u>ic</u>

ce **ram** <u>ic</u>

cap *i* <u>tal</u> **is** <u>tic</u>

*char *ac* <u>ter</u> **is** <u>tic</u>

Dem *o* **crat** <u>ic</u>

dip *lo* **mat** <u>ic</u>

dra **mat** <u>ic</u>

e **las** <u>tic</u>

ec *o* **nom** <u>ic</u>

do **mes** <u>tic</u>

e *lec* **tron** <u>ic</u>

em **phat** <u>ic</u>

pan **dem** <u>ic</u>

fa **nat** <u>ic</u>

fan **tas** <u>tic</u>

pes *si* **mis** <u>tic</u>

har **mon** <u>ic</u>

his **tor** <u>ic</u>

mag <u>ic</u>

me **chan** <u>ic</u>

me **lod** <u>ic</u>

cat *as* **tro** <u>phic</u>

op *ti* **mis** <u>tic</u>

ar **tis** <u>tic</u>

par *a* **lyt** <u>ic</u>

i **ner** <u>tia</u>

a **ca** <u>cia</u>

am **bro** <u>sia</u>

an *es* **the** <u>sia</u>

fan **ta** <u>sia</u>

Answers for Multiple Syllable Worksheet 5

com *pa* <u>ny</u>

a **cad** *e* <u>my</u>

en *e* <u>my</u>

ac *tiv* **i** <u>ty</u>

ad **ver** *si* <u>ty</u>

a *gen* <u>cy</u>

a **bil** *i* <u>ty</u>

ac **ces** *si* **bil** *i* <u>ty</u>

a **nat** *o* <u>my</u>

au **thor** *i* <u>ty</u>

a **vail** *a* **bil** *i* ty

but *te* ry

bub <u>bly</u>

ca **la** *mi* ty

cert *i* <u>fy</u>

amp *li* <u>fy</u>

clas *si* fy

dig *ni* <u>fy</u>

sat *is* <u>fy</u>

e **lec** *tri* <u>fy</u>

ex **em** *pli* <u>fy</u>

for *ti* <u>fy</u>

gra *ti* <u>fy</u>

glo *ri* <u>fy</u>

i **den** *ti* <u>fy</u>

jus *ti* <u>fy</u>

mag *ni* <u>fy</u>

no *ti* <u>fy</u>

ab *di* <u>cate</u>

ac **com** *mo* <u>date</u>

ac *ti* <u>vate</u>

mo *ti* <u>vate</u>

ad *vo* <u>cate</u>

af **fec** <u>tion</u> <u>ate</u>

ag *gra* <u>vate</u>

ag *i* <u>tate</u>

con **sid** e <u>rate</u>

cer **tif** *i* <u>cate</u>

con **sol** e <u>date</u>

dec *o* <u>rate</u>

Answers for Multiple Syllable Worksheet 6

grat *i* <u>tude</u>

at *ti* <u>tude</u>

lon *gi* <u>tude</u>

lat *i* <u>tude</u>

sol *i* <u>tude</u>

al *ti* <u>tude</u>

mag *ni* <u>tude</u>

ar <u>tist</u>

bo *ta* <u>nist</u>

col *o* nist

cyc <u>list</u>

e **col** *o* <u>gist</u>

fi *na* <u>list</u>

flo <u>rist</u>

for *ma* <u>list</u>

lob <u>by</u> <u>ist</u>

in *ter* <u>nist</u>

op *ti* <u>mist</u>

psy **cho** *lo* gist

stig *ma* <u>tism</u>

ac *ti* <u>vism</u>

cri *ti* cism

au <u>tism</u>

an **tag** *o* <u>nist</u>

pro **tag** *o* <u>nist</u>

min *i* <u>mal</u> <u>ist</u>

po **di** *a* <u>trist</u>

act i vist

re **cep** <u>tion</u> <u>ist</u>

nu **tri** <u>tion</u> <u>ist</u>

Answers for Multiple Syllable Worksheet 7

mu <u>sic</u>	*com* **bus** <u>tion</u>	**con** *sul* **ta** <u>tion</u>
fu *tur* **is** <u>tic</u>	*sug* **ges** <u>tion</u>	**jur** *is* **dic** <u>tion</u>
pub <u>lic</u>	*con* **junc** <u>tion</u>	**spec** *u* **la** <u>tion</u>
re **pub** <u>lic</u>	*con* **grat** *u* **la** <u>tion</u>	**con** *tri* **bu** <u>tion</u>
rus <u>tic</u>	**grad** *u* **a** <u>tion</u>	*u* **til** *i* <u>ty</u>
ul *tra* **so** <u>nic</u>	**cons** *ti* **tu** <u>tion</u>	**mal** *nu* **tri** <u>tion</u>
ab **duc** tion	*per* **cus** <u>sion</u>	**stim** *u* **la** <u>tion</u>
ac **cu** *mu* **la** tion	*pro* **pul** <u>sion</u>	*u* **ni** **for** *mi* <u>ty</u>
ac *cu* **sa** <u>tion</u>	*trans* **fu** <u>sion</u>	**for** *tu* <u>nate</u>
fu <u>sion</u>	*se* **clu** <u>sion</u>	
	mu **si** <u>cian</u>	

Answers for Multiple Syllable Worksheet 8

pic <u>ture</u>

ad **ven** <u>ture</u>

de **par** <u>ture</u>

fur **ni** <u>ture</u>

struc <u>ture</u>

cul <u>ture</u>

sub **cul** <u>ture</u>

temp *er* **a** <u>ture</u>

Answers for Multiple Syllable Worksheet 9

stu **pen** <u>dous</u>

a **non** *y* <u>mous</u>

bois *te* <u>rous</u>

cal <u>lous</u>

car **niv** *o* <u>rous</u>

co **nif** *e* <u>rous</u>

con **spic** *u* <u>ous</u>

fa <u>mous</u>

con **tin** *u* <u>ous</u>

dan *ger* <u>ous</u>

fab *u* lous

gen *er* <u>ous</u>

haz *ar* <u>dous</u>

jeal <u>ous</u>

joy <u>ous</u>

en **or** <u>mous</u>

lu *min* <u>ous</u>

tu **mul** *tu* <u>ous</u>

vil *lain* <u>ous</u>

tre **men** <u>dous</u>

mo **men** <u>tous</u>

Answers for Multiple Syllable Worksheet 10

an *ni* **ver** <u>sary</u>

ca <u>nary</u>

boun <u>dary</u>

burg <u>lary</u>

con **tem** *po* <u>rary</u>

con <u>trary</u>

dic tion <u>ary</u>

com *pli* **men** <u>tary</u>

dig *ni* <u>tary</u>

cul *i* <u>nary</u>

he **re** *di* <u>tary</u>

cus *to* <u>mary</u>

hon *o* rary

glos <u>sary</u>

frag *men* <u>tary</u>

ex *tra* **or** *di* <u>nary</u>

cat *e* <u>gory</u>

cir **cu** *la* <u>tory</u>

com **pul** <u>sory</u>

con *tra* **dic** <u>tory</u>

fac <u>tory</u>

his <u>tory</u>

in *tro* **duc** <u>tory</u>

me *mo* <u>ry</u>

la **bor** *a* <u>tory</u>

sat *is* **fac** <u>tory</u>

vic <u>tory</u>

ac *cu* <u>racy</u>

can *di* <u>dacy</u>

con **spir** <u>acy</u>*

del *i* <u>cacy</u>

de **moc** <u>racy</u>

di **plo** <u>macy</u>*

pri <u>vacy</u>

ad *vo* <u>cacy</u>

fal <u>lacy</u>

in **ac** *cu* <u>racy</u>

lit *er* <u>acy</u>

the **oc** <u>racy</u>

Answers for Multiple Syllable Worksheet 11

al **fal** <u>fa</u>

al *ge* <u>bra</u>*

bal *ler* **i** <u>na</u>*

bo **log** <u>na</u>

ban **dan** <u>a</u>*

gum <u>bo</u>

ha <u>lo</u>

mos **quit** <u>o</u>*

Am *a* <u>zon</u>

ap <u>ron</u>

ba <u>con</u>

ba <u>ton</u>

bec <u>kon</u>

bi <u>son</u>

ab **dom** *i* <u>nal</u>*

ad **di** <u>tion</u> <u>al</u>

ac *tu* <u>al</u>

al **pha** *be* **ti** <u>cal</u>

Answers for Multiple Syllable Worksheet 12

ve *ter* <u>an</u>

be <u>gan</u>

car *a* <u>van</u>

car *di* <u>gan</u>

pe <u>can</u>

pel *i* <u>can</u>

work <u>man</u>

watch <u>man</u>

ap **pro** <u>val</u>

bi *fo* <u>cal</u>

bri <u>dal</u>

bru <u>tal</u>

bo **tan** *i* <u>cal</u>

sym <u>bol</u>

con **ven** <u>tion</u> <u>al</u>

ma **the** *mat* **i** <u>cal</u>

hor *i* **zon** <u>tal</u>

phe **no** *me* <u>nal</u>

re **la** <u>tion</u> <u>al</u>

ec *o* **nom** *i* <u>cal</u>

Answers for Multiple Syllable Worksheet 13

am mo nia*

bac *ter* ia

cri ter ia

mem o *ra* bil ia

mag nol ia

triv ia

u top ia*

sub ur bia

se pia

hys *ter* ia

ra *di* o

pa *ti* o

po *li* o

stu di o

scen ar i o

am phi *bi* an

ci vi *li* an

co me *di* an

cus to *di* an

his tor *i* an

guar *di* an

li brar *i* an

me rid *i* an

thes pi an

on i on

mil li on

bil li on

bul li on

cen tu *ri* on

com pa *ni* on

do mi *ni* on

o pi *ni* on

pa vi *li* on

u *ni* on

re u *ni* on

scor *pi* on

ar ter *i* al

bac ter *i* al

bi en *ni* al

bron *chi* al

bur *i* al

me dal *li* on

mi *ni* on

cer e mo *ni* al

co lo *ni* al

e *di* to *ri* al

ma ter *i* al

in dus *tri* al

me *di* al

ser *i* al

mi cro *bi* al

mil len *ni* al

tes *ti* mo *ni* al

ter *ri* to *ri* al

cra ni al

im per *i* al

me mo *ri* al

ra *di* al

Answers for Multiple Syllable Worksheet 14

ce **les** <u>tial</u>

con *fi* **den** <u>tial</u>

es **sen** <u>tial</u>

im **par** <u>tial</u>

i **ni** <u>tial</u>

mar <u>tial</u>

sub **stan** <u>tial</u>

par <u>tial</u>

po *ten* <u>tial</u>

pre *si* **den** <u>tial</u>

re **si** *den* <u>tial</u>

se **quen** <u>tial</u>

tor **ren** <u>tial</u>

be *ne* **fi** <u>cial</u>

gla <u>cial</u>

fi **nan** <u>cial</u>

com **mer** <u>cial</u>

of **fi** <u>cial</u>

ju **di** <u>cial</u>

sa *cri* **fi** <u>cial</u>

Answers for Multiple Syllable Worksheet 15

ac <u>cent</u>

ac *ci* <u>dent</u>

a **gree** <u>ment</u>

a **part** <u>ment</u>

co **in** *ci* <u>dent</u>

com <u>ment</u>

com *pe* <u>tent</u>*

con <u>sent</u>

com *pli* <u>ment</u>*

el *e* <u>ment</u>

do *cu* <u>ment</u>

ab <u>sence</u>

cir **cum** *fer* <u>ence</u>

com <u>mence</u>

con *fer* <u>ence</u>*

con *se* <u>quence</u>*

con **sis** <u>tence</u>

ex **is** <u>tence</u>

ex **cel** <u>lence</u>

in *fer* <u>ence</u>

in **sis** <u>tence</u>

in *no* <u>cence</u>

in *flu* <u>ence</u>

sci <u>ence</u>

cir **cum** *fer* <u>ence</u>

au *di* <u>ence</u>

con **ve** *ni* <u>ence</u>

ex **per** *i* <u>ence</u>

re **si** *li* **ence**

con **ve** *ni* <u>ent</u>

ex **pe** *di* <u>ent</u>

re **ci** *pi* <u>ent</u>

in *con* **ve** *ni* <u>ent</u>

nu *tri* <u>ent</u>

in **gre** *di* <u>ent</u>

le *ni* <u>ent</u>

re **si** *li* <u>ent</u>

o **ri** <u>ent</u>

o **be** *di* <u>ent</u>

Sample Goals

Given five each CVC words, xxx will spell 80% of the words correctly on two samples

Given five each CCVC words, xxx will spell 80% of the words correctly on two samples

Given five each CVCC words, xxx will spell 80% of the words correctly on two samples

Given three minutes and a topic xxx will write a paragraph spelling 80% of the CVC words written correctly on two samples.

Given three minutes and a topic xxx will write a paragraph spelling 80% of the CCVC words written correctly on two samples

Given three minutes and a topic xxx will write a paragraph spelling 80% of the CVCC words written correctly on two samples

Given ten CVC words, student will correctly decode 80% on two samples

Given ten CCVC words, student will correctly decode 80% on two samples

Given ten CVCC words, student will correctly decode 80% on two samples

Given five sentences containing primarily CVC words, student will correctly decode 80% on two samples

Given five sentences containing primarily CCVC words, student will correctly decode 80% on two samples

Given five sentences containing primarily CVCC words, student will correctly decode 80% on two samples

Given ten CVC words, student will correctly d spell 80% on two samples

Given ten CCVC words, student will correctly spell 80% on two samples

Given ten CVCC words, student will correctly spell 80% on two samples

Given five sentences containing primarily CVC words, student will correctly encode 80% on two samples

Given five sentences containing primarily CCVC words, student will correctly encode 80% on two samples

Given five sentences containing primarily CVCC words, student will correctly encode 80% on two samples

Sample Objectives

Given five CVC words student will segment, delete one sound to create a new word

Given five words student will change one sound to create a new word

Given five CVC words student will spell 4 of 5 of the words correctly on two samples

Given ten CVC words student will correctly track the phoneme changes on 8 of 10 on two samples

Given five CCVC words student will segment, delete one sound to create a new word

Given five CCVC words student will change one sound to create a new word

Given five CCVC words student will spell 4 of 5 of the words correctly on two samples

Given ten CCVC words student will correctly track the phoneme changes on 8 of 10 on two samples

Given five CVCC words student will segment, delete one sound to create a new word

Given five CVCC words student will change one sound to create a new word

Given five CVCC words student will spell 4 of 5 of the words correctly on two samples

Given ten CVCC words student will correctly track the phoneme changes on 8 of 10 on two samples

Given five CCVC words student will segment, delete one sound to create a new word, change one sound to create a new word, and spell 80% of the words correctly on two samples

Given five CVCC words student will segment, delete one sound to create a new word, change one sound to create a new word, and spell 80% of the words correctly on two samples

Given five short vowel words ending with the /k/ sound, the student will spell four of five correctly on two samples

Given five long vowel words ending with the /k/ sound, the student will spell 4 of 5 correctly on two samples

Given five mixed vowel words ending with the /k/ sound, the student will spell 4 of 5 correctly on two samples

Given five short vowel words ending with the /ch/ sound, the student will spell 4 of 5 correctly on two samples

Given five long vowel words ending with the /ch/ sound, the student will spell 4 of 5 correctly on two samples

Given five mixed vowel words ending with the /ch/ sound, the student will spell 4 of 5 correctly on two samples

Given five short vowel words ending with the /j/ sound, the student will spell 4 of 5 correctly on two samples

Given five long vowel words ending with the /j / sound, the student will spell 4 of 5 correctly on two samples

Given five mixed vowel words ending with the /j/ sound, the student will spell 4 of 5 correctly on two samples

Given five CVC words student will delete one sound to create a new word correctly for 4 of 5 words on two samples

Given five CCVC words student will delete one sound to create a new word correctly for 4 of 5 words on two samples

Given five CVCC words student will delete one sound to create a new word correctly for 4 of 5 words on two samples

Given five sets of segmented CVC phonemes student will repeat and blend the phonemes to figure out the word correctly for 4 of 5 on two samples

Given five sets of segmented CCVC phonemes student will repeat and blend the phonemes to figure out the word correctly for 4 of 5 on two samples

Given five sets of segmented CVCC phonemes student will repeat and blend the phonemes to figure out the word correctly for 4 of 5 on two samples

Given a xxx level passage of xxx length to read, xxx will correctly read xx% of the words having 3 to 5 syllables on xx trials

Given 5 sentences with 2 or more words having 3 to 5 syllables, xxxx will read and write the words in the sentences with xxx% accuracy reading and XX% accuracy spelling the multiple syllable words on 4 of 5 sentences

Given 10 words ending with xxx, xxx will correctly read xx of 10 on xx consecutive trials

Given 10 words ending with xxx, xxx will correctly spell xx of 10 on xx consecutive trials

Glossary

NOTE: Underlined words are the 'professional' vocabulary of teachers and speech language pathologists and provided to the home school parent for clarification and support. The letters listed on each page of lists will provide you with enough information to teach your child using the process outlined.

alphabetic principle: the concept that letters and patterns of letters are symbols that represent sounds

alveolar: sounds produced when the tongue touches or is near the alveolar gum ridge behind the front teeth:/t/ /d/ /n/ /l/ /s/ /z/

auditory: refers to hearing; information that one hears, pertaining to that part of the nervous system that processes information received through the ears

auditory discrimination: refers to determining fine differences between signals of information received through the ears or heard

auditory tracking: in this work refers to determining changes between the sequence of phonemes or discriminating changes in individual phonemes between syllables [i.e., crab vs. carb or pat vs. pit]

bade: old English word that is past tense for 'bid' as in "said goodbye".

bide: wait, take your time

bilk: cheat someone of their money through trickery

bleat: sound made by a sheep

blem: a blemish

blend, blending: combine, tie together; in this work, combining sounds to figure out a word

bod: slang for 'body'

boon: a bonus, or blessing

bop: to hit, often on the head —"Little Bunny FooFoo hopping through the forest picking up the field mice and bopping them on the head"

bot: piece of software that can execute commands

botch: to mess something up

bro: slang for 'brother'

ccvc: consonant-consonant-vowel-consonant

ccvcc: consonant-consonant-vowel-consonant-consonant

chock: from olden times when people used wagons. They put a wedge of wood against a wheel [called a chock] to keep it from moving.

cleat: a piece of metal shaped like a 'T' for wrapping rope around. Often found on a boat.

consonant: a sound or letter representing a sound that is formed by shaping or obstructing the air flow [any letter that is not a vowel]

cray: short for crayfish; or short for crazy

creed: a statement of belief

cud: partly digested food that a cow chews

cvc: consonant-vowel-consonant

cvcc: consonant-vowel-consonant-consonant

dap: style of fishing; let the fly bob touch the water, but do not let the line touch the water

decoding: assign sounds to letters in a pattern to figure out a written word

deleting: take away; in this work it refers to taking away a sound [i.e., Blake, bake, lake}

dell: a small valley as in "The Farmer in the Dell"

dentals: sounds made in combination with the lips and teeth: /f/ /v/ /th/

dictate or dictation: tell someone what to write or the act of telling someone what to write

digraph: two letters that represent one sound - ph for /f/, ai for long vowel /a/, etc.

din: noise

diagraph: two letters for one vowel sound.

diphthong: They are simply vowels that move your mouth around. When we say /oy/ as in 'boy' our mouth 'scoots' from the /o/ sound to the /ee/ sound. /a/ scoots from /e/ to /ee/. There are 8 sounds like this. Try to feel your mouth move as you say the vowel sounds in these words: 'down' 'boy' 'ate' 'light' 'few' 'boat' 'air' 'sure' /oy/ /oi/ /ou/ /ow/ /ew/ /ar/ /or//air/ and /ear/.

encoding: to write letters, syllables in sequence to represent the sounds in words

flea: insect

flee: run away; Flee and flea are included here as an example of how the use of diphthongs helps the reader to understand word meanings.

floss: acronym for the doubling of consonants after a short vowel in a one syllable word -double f, l, and s after a short vowel

Fram: name of a company that makes air filters for cars

fraught: full of something - usually has a negative connotation such as 'danger'

fray: threads separating or pulling away from the edge of cloth

gad: run around

isolate or isolation: separate something by itself; in this work separating a unit of sound from others in a syllable

labials: sounds made with the lips: /p/ /b/ /w/ /m/

lob: throw or toss

long vowels: sound like letter names.

lop: cut off

lull: a pause to sleep, relax, be quiet

mod: modern

mull: think something over

nib: pointed part of a pen where the ink comes out; a small piece of something like candy or corn

oral motor placement: using language to describe and associate the sound that is elicited to the placement and shaping of the tongue, teeth, lips, and jaw.

palatals: sounds produced when the tongue is raised toward the palate, or roof of the mouth: /y/ as in yes [requires a gliding movement of the jaw--the student may interpret two phonemes for this movement. Teach that it is a gliding movement having one letter]

palatal-alveolar: sounds elicited with the tongue high and close to the hard palate and pulled back slightly yet near the alveolar ridge: /r/ /sh/ /ch/ and /j/ as in judge/. The /zh/ sound, as in the word treasure, is also in this group; however, it is not included in the pages of this book.

pawn: a piece in a chess game

pesk: one who annoys or agitates

phoneme: an individual unit of sound within a syllable

phonemic processing: refers to the auditory system's ability to segment phonemes. People who are proficient in the area of phonemic processing can count the number of phonemes and say each sound in isolation.

phonological processing: refers to the ability to understand that sentences are comprised of separate words, process the space, or break between words in an auditory signal, and the break between syllables in words. People proficient in the area phonological processing can count words in sentences and syllables in words; they are able to determine the ending of a sentence and the separation point between syllables.

pip: break through the shell of an egg; what a bird does when it hatches.

pith: spongy tissue in the center of a stem of a plant

plea: an appeal, a legal term for an appeal or attempt to defend

pod: the outside of a pea when it grows on a plant; compartment of a building

pog: a game played by flipping over small, flat cardboard disks

pro: short for professional

prone: likely to do something; or lying flat on the floor

rad: abbreviation for radius

reversal: change to opposite direction

rut: boring routine, long deep track usually made in the wet ground from tires

segmenting: separating

sequencing: in specific order

short vowels: are tones or phonemes produced in the front of the mouth from top [closed] to bottom [open] {short i, e, a, u, o}

slay: to kill

slew: to have a lot of something or past tense of slay

smidge: a little bit

spay: neuter a cat or dog

spew: to spit out

stake: wood or metal stick placed in the ground for a tent or fence

steak: cut of meat --- the words stake and steak are included to demonstrate how alternate spellings of words that sound the same helps the reader to understand word meanings.

syllable: unit of connected sounds within a word

tad: a little bit

tare: an old English word meaning 'weed'

tink: emit a high pitched noise such as a 'chirp'

tog: coat or cloak

tome: big, thick book

tot: small child

velars: sounds produced in the back of the mouth using the soft palate: /k/ /g/ /ng/

word family: a group of words that share a common base -i.e., might, fight, right; file, mile, pile

writ: a written command; word often used in legal documents.

Bibliography

https://www.ncbi.nlm.nih.gov/pubmed/27764410 abstract found here
https://www.researchgate.net/publication/248844092_Theory-Guided_Spelling_Assessment_and_Intervention_A_Case_Study/citation/download
Apel, Kenn and Masterson, Julie "Theory-Guided Spelling Assessment and Intervention: A Case Study"

Kenn Apel*,1 , Julie J. Masterson2 "Comparing the Spelling and Reading Abilities of Students with Cochlear Implants and Students with Typical Hearing"; Journal of Deaf Studies and Deaf Education, 2015, 125–135; doi:10.1093/deafed/env002 Advance Access publication February 17, 2015, Empirical Manuscript

Kenn Apel and Julie J. Masterson featured Language Speech and Hearing Services in the Schools July 2001, Vol. 32, 182-195. doi:10.1044/0161-1461(2001/017)

Bashir, Anthony S. Writing and Academic Resources Center, Emerson College, Boston, MA; Pamela E. Hook The MGH Institute of Health Professions, Boston, MA "Fluency: A Key Link Between Word Identification and Comprehension" LANGUAGE, SPEECH, AND HEARING SERVICES IN SCHOOLS • Vol. 40 • 196–200 • April 2009

Burns, Martha, Ph.D. "Auditory Processing Disorders, Dyslexia and Apraxia: Assessments and Evidence-Based Interventions- Review of Neuroscience Applications and APD"

Burns, Martha Ph.D. "Training Auditory Processing in Children with Autism Spectrum Disorders and other Developmental Disabilities," https://www.northernspeech.com f

DeHaene, Stanislas, "READING IN THE BRAIN" Copyright © 2009 by Stanislas Dehaene.

Dowhower, Sarah L. "Repeated reading: Research into practice" Article reports on the benefits of repeated reading, various ways to conduct repeated reading exercises, and classroom applications of repeated reading.

Fair, Ginnie Chase and Combs, Dorie. "Nudging Fledgling Teen Readers from the Nest: From Round Robin to Real Reading" The Clearing House, 84:224-230, 2011 Copyright Taylor & Francis Group, LLC ISSN: 0009-8655 prin; 1939-912x online DOIL 1).1080/00098655.2011.575417

Gillon, Gail (solr/searchresults.aspx?author=Gail+Gillon) and Barbara Dodd (solr/searchresults.aspx?author=Barbara+Dodd) "The Effects of Training Phonological, Semantic, and Syntactic Processing Skills in Spoken Language on Reading Ability" Language, Speech, and Hearing Services in Schools, January 1995, Vol. 26, 58-68. doi:10.1044/0161-1461.2601.58

Joshi, R Maletesha; Treiman, Rebecca; Carreker, Suzanne, and Moats, Louisa C. "How Words Cast Their Spell" Masterson, Julie; Apel, Kenn "Linking Characteristics Discovered in Spelling Assessment to Intervention Goals and Methods" Learning Disability Quarterly Vol. 33, No. 3, SPELLING (Summer 2010) pp. 185-198

Meyer, Mariane S., and Felton Rebecca H. "Repeated Reading to Enhance Fluency: Approaches and New Directions" Annals of Dyslexia, Vol. 49, 1999 Copyright 1999 by the International Dyslexia Association ISSN 0736-9387   May be found at:

Turken, And U., Dronkers, Nina F. "The Neural Architecture of the Language Comprehension Network: Converging Evidence from Lesion and Connectivity Analyses" Frontiers in Systems Neuroscience published online February 10, 2011.

Masterson, Julie . Classroom Implementation of the Multilinguistic Model for Literacy Instruction, Missouri State University Literacy Lab
http://nebula.wsimg.com/5cf5abb73bba3ac04502e87b4af9909a?AccessKeyId=E197AE8D5240BD028530&disposition=0&alloworigin=1

Jeanne Wanzek, Brandy Gatlin, Stephanie Al Otaiba & Young-Suk Grace Kim "The Impact of Transcription Writing Interventions for First-Grade Students" Pages 1-16 | Published online: 20 Dec 2016

National Reading Panel (2000). Teaching children to read: An evidence-based assessment of the scientific research literature on reading and its implications for reading instruction
https://www.nichd.nih.gov/sites/default/files/publications/pubs/nrp/Documents/report.pdf

NAEP 2019 National Report Card for 4th grade Reading
https://www.nationsreportcard.gov/reading/nation/achievement/?grade=4

Psyche Loui,[1,*] Kenneth Kroog,[2] Jennifer Zuk,[1] Ellen Winner,[2,3] and Gottfried Schlaug[1] Relating Pitch Awareness to Phonemic Awareness in Children: Implications for Tone-Deafness and Dyslexia

Quick Nancy and Erickson Karen "A Multilinguistic Approach to Evaluating Student Spelling in Writing Samples " Language, Speech, and Hearing Services in Schools, July 2018, Vol. 49, 509-523. doi:10.1044/2018_LSHSS-17-0095

Robertson,Carolyn, M.Ed. and Salter, Wanda, MS. CCC-SLP. Phonological Awareness Test 2 (PAT 2)

Sprenger-Charolles, Liliane, Colé, Pascale Fields, R Douglas "Change in Brain's White Matter" Science Vol 330, 5 November2010 May be found at:

 Winskel, Heather The effects of an early history of otitis media on children's language and literacy skill development Article in British Journal of Educational Psychology · January 2007

Velluntino, Frank and Scanlon, Donna M. "Phonological Coding, Phonological Awareness and Reading Ability: Evidence from a Longitudinal and Experimental Study."

ABOUT THE AUTHOR

Early in her career struggling readers and writers captured Vickie's attention. She developed a focused interest in phonology, phonemic processing, and language-based reading disabilities. She began working part time in public schools in 1973 as a substitute teacher and substitute Speech Therapist. By 1990 she was a full-time Speech Language Pathologist in a rural school district serving K-12. For the past 30 years most students were in grades 3-5, but she also worked with students in preschool through 12th grade. Now she provides speech therapy to virtual school students part time through video conferencing.

As time passed, she developed a system for helping children to "break the code" and learn to match sounds [phonemes] and letters, put them together to form words, and sort out the many problems they faced with understanding phonics and learning to read faster. After retirement, she wrote her ideas down in the publication "20 Minute Phonemic Training for Dyslexia, Auditory Processing and Spelling." Three years later, she realized that a great deal of information could be added to help the home-school parent and teachers who do not have a strong phonological or speech and language therapy background to apply the strategies and word lists provided in both books. "Winning Solutions for Struggling Readers and Spellers" is the result.

With a significant section of the population reading below 6th grade level, it is her greatest hope that both publications will enable children, through parent or professional instruction to achieve higher reading and spelling competency. It is her hope they will have brighter futures through improved literacy skills.

As a postscript, another piece of information to consider is that multiple ear infections and chronic fluid in the middle ear cause mild intermittent hearing loss. Think of it like trying to hear underwater. When children experience otitis media during their early years when phonemic processing of sounds in words is developing, researchers have found that reading and spelling skills are often adversely affected for many years into elementary school.

The book "How to Blow Your Nose by Little Tiny Elephant" uses story and rhyme to teach children how to clear mucous to help prevent this problem. Authored by Amanda Dinsmore and illustrated by Vickie Dinsmore.

Printed in Great Britain
by Amazon

15721199R00174